REVIEW BLURBS

Incredible book that bridges through a look at major religions following Joseph Campbells Heroes Journey... Though it does have a Christian lens, and the author at least has a deep connection and respect for Jesus, I found this book to be inspiring, thought provoking and a wonderful read.

—Chris Carlson

David Kuby has written an extraordinary synopsis of past and present psychology that paves the way to healthy families and faith. His book is practical and spiritual in the most personal of ways.

—Richard Godfrey- The African Queen, Tales of Motherhood and Wild Bees

I have thoroughly enjoyed reading 'Heroism in the Pursuit of Happiness'. I found the history of the Kuby family fascinating how they managed to navigate through their young lives. They were not only survivors, but they flourished in their adult lives despite their difficult beginnings. Very thought provoking and inspiring.

—Darlene Merritt, St. Louis, Mo.

THE HEROIC RESILIENCE
OF **HAPPINESS**

THE HEROIC RESILIENCE
OF HAPPINESS

Empowering Love thru Life's Pits and Peaks

DAVID KUBY

Copyright © 2023 David Kuby.

All rights reserved. No part of this book may be reproduced, stored, or transmitted by any means—whether auditory, graphic, mechanical, or electronic—without written permission of both publisher and author, except in the case of brief excerpts used in critical articles and reviews. Unauthorized reproduction of any part of this work is illegal and is punishable by law.

ISBN: 979-8-89031-495-6 (sc)
ISBN: 979-8-89031-496-3 (hc)
ISBN: 979-8-89031-497-0 (e)

Because of the dynamic nature of the Internet, any web addresses or links contained in this book may have changed since publication and may no longer be valid. The views expressed in this work are solely those of the author and do not necessarily reflect the views of the publisher, and the publisher hereby disclaims any responsibility for them.

One Galleria Blvd., Suite 1900, Metairie, LA 70001
(504) 702-6708

CONTENTS

Book Summary vii

Preface to the book ix

Dedication of the book and Thanksgiving xiii

Synopsis xv

Chapter 1 Power and Love Through Our Early Lifespan 1

Chapter 2 Seeking Happiness through Adult Power and Love 13

Chapter 3 Peaks and Pits in Power and Love as We Die 24

Chapter 4 Religious Visions of Divine Power and Love 37

Chapter 5 Happiness Love and Heroic Power for Adler, Freud & Jung 54

Chapter 6 Power vs Love in the Enneagram's Pits and Peaks 66

Chapter 7 Power and Love in Happiness Research 79

Chapter 8 Happiness Through Heroic Virtues: Balanced Resilience Through Life's Pits and Peaks 89

Chapter 9 Balanced Resilience Through Life's Peaks and Pits: The Power and Love of Heroic Mentors for the Kuby Family 109

Chapter 10 The Resilient Power of Faith and Family 137

Preface #1—Why is this book is needed? 155

Preface #2—What are my qualifications to write such a book? ... 159

Bibliography of Happiness, Heroism and Marriage 161

Endnote 167

BOOK SUMMARY

The "pursuit of resilience" requires us to overcome the pits of life to recover life-giving peaks. Before giving birth, the mom-to-be experiences a crisis of pain and loss of control. Suddenly the pit yields to the peak of the miracle of birth and God's unconditional love for the newborn baby even though the newborn brings the chaos of sleepless nights and endless work for a needy, crying wordless newborn who can bring the peaks of joyful smiles from baby to mom. The baby's challenge is to find "secure attachment" to a very present mom in order to avert the pit of mistrust and achieve the goal of ongoing trust for an abiding inner security through the ups (peaks) and downs (pits) of life.

For the largest part of our lifespan, our trust in life is through the experience of God's forgiveness and persistent love despite our mistakes, selfishness and defiant disobedience seen well through the teen years but better disguised as we "mature" to meet the immediate challenges we face. We need competence to succeed in life so we learn the required discipline of our careers. We need to be socialized into the give-and-take trust of marriage beyond the idealized peak of romance into real intimacy, to "stand in love" as a devoted commitment rather than to rely upon the ups and downs of romantic feelings which can make us "fall out of love" with our mate. We can and do need to "fall out of love" with ourselves as #one and surrender to God's higher love and secure attachment. We learn to stay attached in our hearts to our missing adult children during the midlife "empty nest" until we celebrate our new connection as grandparents to the next generation to revisit the lifespan again once removed from parenting pressures.

By midlife, our careers have reached their peak in achievement and power, until our sun slowly sets into retirement . As seniors, we see the overview of the peaks and pits of our success and failures, joys and sorrows and seek the resilience that changes possible despair into acceptance of our life as a whole. Just as birth had its pain and loss of control, the leaving our physical bodies may have these same pits followed by the similar joyful celebration as our souls are reborn into an eternity of God's complete forgiveness and unconditional love through the sacrifice of Christ's death and resurrection wherein human resilience is made perfect. We have glimpses of our final rebirth through the crises of all our eight stages of our lifespan until we can finally see the full truth of this mystery. Why not celebrate with gratitude every rebound in our lives from pits to peaks?

PREFACE TO THE BOOK

The thrust of the first half of the lifespan appears that we are getting more powerful and more loving as we grow from early childhood into midlife, but the rise is followed by a decline. We see that our careers often peak at midlife and then decline lower than the state we would wish from the high point of our life and that the physical descent into old age and death looks like we missed the happiness train altogether. Only a minority of life's pilgrims are immortalized through induction into some timeless Hall of Fame or Sainthood while the rest of us live on through the genetic mix of our offspring and largely forgotten in any of the modest career achievements we may have had. However many happy stops we have along life's way, we need to grasp the final destination of this train to have the needed spiritual fitness for this journey.

*With our eyes opened to reality, we realize that every "pit" stop of our journey is a preview of our final destiny. Buddhists see each of these "pits" as the "suffering" that comes with our experiential encounters with "impermanence". One remedy is to find ever greater levels of "permanence" with the footsteps of the Buddha as a guide. Christians understand the "pits" of life as the inevitable small crosses of life before the final cross of death. For both Buddhists and Christians, the pits of life provide a classroom for the development of the spiritual fitness needed to pass the final test to graduate beyond death into eternal life. The big difference is the personal encounter Christians have during their painful crosses as described by Albert Schweitzer. "He comes to us as One unknown...(and) reveals Himself (to both the wise and the simple) in the **toils, the conflicts, the sufferings** that they shall pass through in His fellowship. And, as an ineffable mystery, they shall learn in their own experience **who HE** is." (Schweitzer, Quest 1910/98, p.403)*

The Buddhist way follows the impersonal, non-theistic law-based methods of science but the Christian way is "an ineffable mystery" which gives us the intimate compassion of divine "fellowship" with a personal God who "reveals himself to us during our journeys through the pits of frustrating "toils, conflicts, sufferings".

In embracing the cross of Christ, the Christian finds both God's loving forgiveness and resurrection power into eternal life - an offer hard to refuse but it takes "faith". Faith, love, forgiveness and resilience jump out as essentials to the Christian induction into spiritual fitness. The Buddhist virtues of spiritual fitness are complementary in the Christian walk familiar through the detachment and mindfulness required in the twelve step program to become free of the bondage of addictions. The Buddhist path makes a coordinated whole of right thinking, right attitudes, right actions which would lead to the right career and right marriage/family.

One spectrum of character types as categorized by the Enneagram's nine types has a combination of virtues and vices which require an integration for the authenticity of integrity and coherent wholeness.

Facing the bondage of our vices takes **courage, honesty and humility** which are the basis of the heroism needed for spiritual fitness. We must battle against our lower self which falls prey to fear, deception and pride. As we seek liberation from the forces that keep us in bondage, we can compensate with the natural virtues of our character type. When our will power fails, we seek a 12 step program that directs us to surrender our false control to our Higher Power above the little addictions that rob our power. Totally ruined lives have been changed from a powerless isolated self to a self empowered by a connection to God as best they can know the intelligent source of power and love in the Universe.

The life span shows the alteration between dependent connection and independent autonomy until there is an integration of the two in the intimate mutuality and greater wholeness of marriage. If we continue this same dynamic in the spiritual realm, our loss of power with age allows us to empower God into our daily lives for a greater intimacy. As our power decreases, God's power increases and we are as connected to God as a baby is to his mother in loving, trusting dependency. Could it be that each of the lifespan tasks challenge us into an installment plan of virtues to prepare us for that final utter dependency of dying to the body to be reborn into a spiritual self? The journey we begin now seeks to answer Zorba when he faced a tragic death: "Where do we come from and where do we go to?"

Outline and Synopsis of the Book in Nine Chapters

Preface: Heroism in the Pursuit of Happiness
ch. 1—Power and love in our Early Lifespan
ch.2—Seeking Happiness through Adult Power and Love
ch. 3—Peaks and Pits in Power and Love as We Die
ch. 4—Divine Power and Love in Religious Revelations
ch. 5—Happiness Love and Heroic Power for Freud, Adler and Jung
ch 6—Power and Love in the Enneagram's Peaks and Pits
ch 7—Power and Love in Happiness Research
ch 8—Happiness Through Heroic Virtue to Resilience
ch. 9—Balanced Resilience through Life's Peaks and Pits (Photos to be integrated)

Our first chapter explores the dynamics of love and power as seen in an overview of the pre-adult (five) stages of the lifespan

Our second chapter focuses on the integration of love and power in marriage and family from young adulthood through midlife into the senior stage of life.

In the third chapter, challenges to power and love are explored in the final stage of the lifespan in some detail including recurrent patterns in the over 8,000 cases of Near Death Experiences.

The fourth chapter looks at the capacity of religious revelation to answer questions on moral goodness in relation to the losses of power and love in the death and dying processes,

In the fifth chapter Freud's view on love and Adler's view on power are explored as well as their differences on the role of religion in happiness. Carl Jung looks at the integration of love and power into wholeness as a deeper religious dimension of the unconscious transformation into a Higher Self,

In Chapter six, the motivations of love vs power is studied in nine different personality/character types of the **"Enneagram"** as they seek to integrate their weaknesses and strengths for honest transparency in marriage and friendship.

Chapter seven reviews selected studies in the interplay between happiness and moral heroism (virtue) in positive psychology research.

Chapter eight is a summary of the book focused on the heroic virtues needed to achieve resilience between pit and peaks to integrate the ups and downs of downs of life through balanced positivity.

Chapter nine provides an illustrated case study of resilience between pits and peaks of one family.

Only this "boots on the ground" personal path through the shared lifespan landscape will bring relevant truth to the theories and generalizations,

The contents of this book have been developed in training psychotherapists both in supervision and in university classes but hopefully this is a type of "self-help" book for everyone motivated to gain perspective on the roles of power and love in all the ups and downs of our lifespan journey.

DEDICATION OF THE BOOK AND THANKSGIVING

This book is dedicated to my wife Gail for adding her first hand experience to this lifespan journey. Not only did Gail share the teaching of Lifespan and Marriage courses at our university for most of a decade as a Nurse, but she continues to be "Nanny Gail" (and "Nena") to families from birth through middle school to confirm the lifespan stage theory with current living examples with her longterm three twosomes. Thus this book is dedicated to my beloved wife and lifespan companion, Gail, for her faith, love and integrity in all the adventures we have shared with each other, our adult children and our grandchildren celebrating their different ages and stages.

Thanks to Barb and Tom for the initial financial investment for the start of this book. Thanks to the library at Holy Names University where I did most of my writing and to the librarian at JFK Berkeley for the first run-off of the entire book in its first draft. Thanks to my students at Patten University and Holy Names who inspired the content and for the heroes in my life who were examples of integrity named in the writer's entry in appendix.

SYNOPSIS

Power and Love through Life's Peaks and Pits: A Vision of the Whole from Birth Through Life to Death and Beyond

What is the right road to take for the pursuit of happiness? Better have a map of the overview with its final destination in view. We begin here with a rough draft overview of our journey ahead focusing on the interplay of power and love as we pursue the happiness goals through the peaks and pits of life's different stages.

An infant's happiness goal is gaining "secure attachment" through the right fit with the primary caretaker (usually mom). In our early lifespan growth, we are "practicing" both in love and power (ch. 1) until the two are fulfilled in different ways during the young, middle and late adult stages (ch. 2). The gold standard achievements during childhood that are most lasting are **secure attachment** from consistent parental love and **achieving competence** through the right genes, right teachers, right learning environments. The more parts that are not right, the higher the requirement for heroism underwritten by our "higher power" to swim against the tide.

The pursuit of happiness requires an integral mix of both power and love. We need love to draw us upward to each peak of happiness through the eight stages of our lifespan. To sustain our climb upward, we need the power of the right effort and the courage to endure the down times of pits. If happiness is understood as a lasting fulfillment as we achieve our lifespan benchmark goals, heroism can be seen as the power of our character virtues to enable these achievements.

We seek to go up the job ladder during the young adult years until we reach our peak and level off. At our plateau, we then mentor the next generation to help them fulfill their potential. For example, a good basketball player may become a good coach to help his team become their best. Ideally the coach and team immortalize themselves by becoming MVP's to become inducted into the hall of fame so that their heroic feats can be remembered and celebrated into their old age and at their deaths. This ideal is what Ernest Becker calls the "immorality project" of the world of sports. Unfortunately, the god of sports championships is fickle as the other teams seek to find the weaknesses of last year's champions to bring them down so far that they may no longer make the playoffs esp. when key players are injured and even coaches deal with their own medical challenges (eg. Golden State's Curry and their coach). Public heroes (sports, the arts, politics) inspire us to practice our own moral heroism both in victories and defeats. Often faithful fans have had to go through years of failures before celebrating a triumphal season. The pits of failures can be the necessary "fertilizer" before a time of true and rich "fruitfulness" causing our roots to grow to a deeper source of life which we will need through the seasons of winter and drought.

Physical death appears as our worst drought and losing season. Rather than rising to the revered tops of our career field and family life, we begin to descend into forced retirements, the loss of intimate spouses, breakdowns with adult children, and losing rather than growing in the social standards of success and status possessions that mark the elite (house, car, clothes, clubs). We may struggle with serious illnesses that limit us physically (with aches and pains) and mentally (forgetfulness, decline of cognitive abilities once a source of pride). We long for paradise but live in the "human condition" which ends with "old age, sickness and death" instead of becoming so good that we are just beamed up into the heaven. As Becker notes, we also live in the "denial of death" pursuing some "immortality project" that will makes us too special to die or leave something behind that outlasts the body that has disappeared into ashes or a grave.

The results of the human condition are well described by Charles Davis.

"Life for the best of us is an untidy mess of unfinished business, broken achievements, personal failures, half successes, short-lived triumphs, belated insights, noble desires and shameful deeds." (Davis, 1982) One life goal is to become our best selves in cultivating virtues to compensate for our vices.

As we examine the reality of death in our journey (ch.3), we realize that the popular and elite culture of scientific secularity have no consoling answers for facing the physical death of the body and no hope for a spiritual continuing life outside the body. Empirical science sees death as the total annihilation of our bodies, our personalities and our world as we know it. This is "the Big Goodbye". You simply leave behind some grief for loved ones, some money, and some memories. Science does not have an adequate paradigm to explain continued existence in a non-physical (unseen) dimension but traditional religious systems do have revelations regarding the afterlife. Why put in so much power and love to book a ticket on the luxurious Titanic? "Swing low Sweet Chariot" I'd rather book a ticket with you because somehow our secular science comes up short where logic fails and truth escapes us. Is the "system rigged against us"? Is the "good news" fake news?

Due to the limits of science, we are forced to seek an alliance with some kind of religious answers (ch. 4) to death. The easiest bridge is to Buddhism which is a non-theistic, cause-effect approach to understand the cause of human suffering. We suffer because we have become attached to something that is not permanent so we suffer with our house built on shifting sand on an earthquake fault falling into shambles. How do we find our way to the solid fault-free Rock? The Buddhist answer is an holistic eightfold lifestyle of living right: from right thinking to right livelihood to detach from addictions which limit freedom and increase the potential of wrongdoing. These are the laws of "Dharma" to follow the Buddha's path to inner peace and happiness which chart virtues vs vices as an ethical system. Vices put us in debt with bad "karma" while virtues increase the good karma of our spiritual bank account to buy into a better life the next time around. Buddhism stays with this world as we know it with harder life circumstances for the spiritually impoverished while the more spiritually fit continually upgrade their life circumstances until they can break free of this cycle into stable happiness of the highest level. This belief in reincarnation has not been proven empirically but is easily adapted into secular new age lifestyles because of its economic parallels shown in the ups and downs of the stock market. The final destination of the karmic journey is the timeless bliss of "Nirvana" achieved by the Buddha and reachable through our higher "Buddha-Self". Comparable to the Buddhist path of virtue is the Jewish righteous path of obedience to God's revealed laws.

The Jewish solution to the problem of death holds that we have an ethical relationship with a personal God who trades our mortal life for eternal life based our ethical pursuit of God's law as children of God. Realizing that we all fall short of true righteousness before the law, the prophets foretold of a Messiah who would redeem the accumulated bad karma of all humanity over history through God's abundant gift of good karma of the highest power given through a loving sacrificial death of a sinless perfect person.

Christianity rose out of Judaism with a leader who claimed to be the long awaited Messiah of Israel, Jesus the Christ, the "Anointed Savior". Christian believers are convinced that the historical Jesus was resurrected from death and that both his death and resurrection are sources of man's rebirth into eternal life. At least 500 witnesses saw the risen Christ over the four weeks following his resurrection before his ascension to his "Heavenly Father". Seculars have difficulty believing in the miracles and resurrection of Christ but have equal difficulty refuting these events. Jesus the Messiah stands out above all men both in love and in power making it impossible to ignore the Christ in a study dedicated to seeing the roles of power and love in pursing happiness and coping with death. Christians prepare for the final "cross" of death by trusting Jesus' power and love through the many little "crosses" (pits) of our normal daily life which they dedicate in love to one Sacred Saving Cross of Christ writ large. The cross at the center of Christian faith goes against our natural pursuit of happiness. Immature young people are sometimes repelled by the inconvenient truths of suffering and death in the reality of our lifespan journey.

Heroism in the Pursuit of Happiness

As you, the reader, take this lifespan journey you may find, as I have found, that you have two companions on either side of your attempted synthesis of modern science and the ancient wisdom path: a secular skeptic and a fully persuaded believer. As you seek your version of a synthesis you may find yourself both challenged positively and judged negatively by both sides as you seek a compromise from what each opposing side sees as ultimate. What can emerge is that all three pilgrims have both higher and lower selves leading each to take different paths by the journey's end. We recall the ancient maxim: "Be humble for we are made of earth. Be noble for we are made of stars." (anonymous) How do we embrace both our common humanity and our shared divinity in true dialogue?

Other than dying itself, the next most challenging stage is the suffering of old age with losses in both love and power. Seniors can become critical of other seniors who are more limited by the aging process as if having to face their own worst self. Seniors may fear pain more than dying, but thank God for the rich data of NDE (Near Death Experiences) which document a release from intolerable pain into a joyful calm and an encounter with a "Being of Light" who is both awesome in power and unconditional in love. As we review our life as a whole, this Christ-like being gives meaning and joy for all of our life's peaks and pits and shows us with humor that we are the ones judging ourselves harshly. The truth of Christ is limited by our own pride mixed with the cultural prejudice of secularity to decrease the power of religion as it increases the power and status of scientific technology. Unanimously all religions agree that God is foremost and all surpassing in the integration of power and love and no human has ever made a better case for the integration of God and man in the person of the historical Jesus. Why do our minds, wills, egos, and secular elitism all resist the person in whom the power of love overcomes the love of power?

*Even the American constitution does not promise us an entitlement to happiness". The only promised right is the "**pursuit** of happiness". This pursuit requires "heroism". Every "promised land" has always been a frontier of challenges and adventures. Similarly our lifespan is a frontier of challenges and adventures requiring courage, a work ethic, honesty and a disciplined determination to fight for truth and goodness. These* *virtues are the "moral heroism" required in the "pursuit" of the happiness since the pursuit requires enduring the pits of frustration, loss, struggle, suffering.*

We are drawn to the "highs" (peaks) in our life's landscapes but not all the peaks are good. The immediate highs of sexual passion, infatuation, drugs or alcohol are among the obvious false peaks that lead us astray. The more subtle false peaks are the highs of pride, elitism, selfishness and other vices that become distortions in love and/or power. We may fear or disdain the pits of failure, humiliation, rejection but these pits may be our best teachers for the virtues of persistence, humility and compassion for those hurting from losses.

The wise "middle path" requires restraint from the allure of false peaks as well as the courage to face the dark pits of creative suffering. The "middle path" of moderation between extremes has been articulated by Aristotle, the Buddha and Christ in different ways. We all must find the middle path that uses our character strengths to offset our moral weaknesses to reach our full potential of becoming our best selves.

We pursue happiness through the two lifespan staples of a longterm love in marriage/family and the longterm achievement of a career and both involve us in communities. We learn to love the other as we love ourselves and to help empower the other as we have learned to be empowered by parents and mentors.

We have completed our summary overview of our entire journey as a map or brief synopsis. Let us now begin at the lifespan beginning seeing the consequences of the love in childhood that gives secure attachment and the competition for power seeking superiority. The "dance" of love and power alternate throughout childhood into the teen vision of a merger of the two in the adult mutuality of marriage where independence vs dependence become interdependence.

CHAPTER ONE

POWER AND LOVE THROUGH OUR EARLY LIFESPAN

1.1—Dependence and Independence in Early Childhood

The co-creation of a child is a marriage of love and power, of the human and the divine, of the mysterious miraculous and the everyday business as usual. Being born and being securely attached are the heroic pursuits of both the mother and child as is the opposite stage of the mom letting go to empower the toddler seeking independent adventures of movement while overseeing safety. We are wired for the original connection that prepares us for the needed attachment to others over one's life. We also have a happiness stage goal for the mastery of movement (crawling, climbing stairs, walking) and for the enjoyment of this empowerment. The pattern of challenge, struggle, and the mastery of tasks at each new stage moves us forward until the striving for power and love merge as young adults become couples, mate and create a family requiring the balance of authority and warmth.

*As humans, we seek both love and power throughout our lifespan as seen in the first two stages of our childhood. The infant wants to passively receive nurturing love from the mother while the toddler wants to assert himself with independent activity. These two opposing drives take turns until finally power **and** love become reconciled into the integrating wholeness of marriage at the young adult stage. The lifespan opposition of* passive dependent love and independent self assertion become reconciled in the interdependent mutuality of marriage which requires both clear boundaries and the growing closeness of intimacy.

We grow because we work to pursue. We learn and adapt as we pursue the specific happiness goals of each lifespan stage, Our inspiration comes from our love of the happiness goals but our pursuit requires the applied power of our wills, our self talk, actions and interactions.

1.2—Freud's View of the Power of Breast-Feeding Baby Love

Freud's biological image of the first stage of nurturing is the mom breastfeeding the baby with skin contact, mutual enjoyment and sufficient time to have a loving interaction. Cross cultural and historical research showed that the Anglo-Saxon Victorians were on the short side of this ideal encounter whereas tropical countries were on the more ideal side leading to inner calm in contrast to the anxiety of Victorian infants. Freud showed some exceptions to the loving breast feeding with some babies biting as teeth came in (power misuse or aggression) and some challenged babies could not attach to the breast with enjoyment because of their stomach distress. A consistent caregiving could still overrule these kinds of breakdowns to achieve "secure attachment" which is the continuing heart of Freud's revelation articulated in "Attachment Theory" which is more amenable to objective, empirical research than Freud's anecdotal therapy case narratives and broad theory.

What is the "secure attachment" that the infant must achieve in order to trust people and the world at large? Secure attachment is "when children feel they can rely on their caregivers to attend to their needs of proximity, emotional support and protection". (E. Erikson) Ruptures in attention are inevitable but the hallmark of a sensitive caregiver is that the ruptures are seen, managed and repaired.

This repair-of-the-rupture factor is good news for parents who are already overly anxious about their competence. Almost half the time there is some distraction for parents to interrupt the ideal attachment, but the damage is repaired when caught and corrected quickly enough in the normal range. Serious breaks happen through either mental illness (eg. depression), some form of drug or alcohol addiction or some grief or loss in the family with a single overwhelmed caregiver.

*The ideal **Happiness** (fulfillment, wellbeing) at the infant stage is achieving love in the form of a "secure attachment" with the mother in the form of loving breast feeding and skin contact over a year or more. Secure attachment existed naturally with the fetus in the womb, disrupted by the separation through the birthing process, and regained as the infant reconnects with the mom "on the other side" connecting by a familiar heart beat, voice, and biochemistry. Intimacy (and trust) are re-established by the caretaker's consistent meeting of the infant's needs discerning the meaning of different forms of crying. Once outside the womb, happiness is no longer an entitlement but a pursuit with the dedicated alliance of parents. The infant may be resistant to connection to the mother because of a colic reaction to the milk or may prefer the ease of bottle milk to the work of breast feeding. Once frustrated the infant may be rejecting of the mother and become insecure as mutuality breaks down on both sides.*

1.3—The Power of Autonomy and Independence for Toddlers

Love is traded for power as the toddler in the "terrible two" stage becomes oppositional ("I say stop but you go, I say yes but you say no") and resistant to parental control almost like an early teenager. Although the toddler's demands for autonomy of movement lack balance, if the parent reacts with their own imbalance seeking control, the toddler's development into freedom of movement may be overly restrictive and leading to self doubt or defiant rebellion. For the toddler, the power of love has been traded for the love of power which could be another ongoing imbalance in later life.

The Toddler's "Neanderthal" demand for power becomes more moderated with preschoolers as their minds develop the capacity for realistic planning and fantasy play but both of these go together into what Freud sees as power manipulation brought into the parental love circle. One parent is favored and the other disliked and seemingly rejected to divide and conquer the unified parental power system. If this continues into life, the person will get entangled with "triangle affairs" and project unfinished love/power messes from their unconscious into "secrets" in the adult world.

After dependency needs are met at the infant stage, the toddler wants the power of independent movements away from the mother as muscles are developed for locomotion. The "love" that was in passively being cared for now becomes a love of muscular movements but with a relative independence. Failure to crawl or walk during the toddler stage will be experienced as self doubt and shame if these forms of autonomy are not achieved.

Riding a two-wheeled bike is an early childhood locomotor empowerment as is learning to drive, getting a license, getting one's first car. Each locomotion increase of empowerment allows the child to teen to move further from parental control with more freedom. At the other end of life, is the senior who is no longer able to pass his driving exam or confined to a wheel chair and must be dependent upon his wife or daughter. Self-determination and autonomy are still important even to seniors and the loss of locomotion autonomy decreases self-esteem. If the needed care giving is done with goodwill by family intimates, new kinds of interdependencies can bring a new chapter of love between seniors and their offspring but the virtues of moral heroism may be needed for the challenges on both sides to keep a positive balance of attitude.

The Toddler stage begins with the muscular power to move and explore independently from their parent's choices. Boys' toys reflect the dream of locomotion power that they have only imperfectly "Thomas the Train" is a popular toy along with toy cars, trucks, airplanes. By contrast, happiness for the girl is being the mom in her own little play house with baby dolls and all the props of home life or playing the bride - connected intimacy more than locomotion but it is empowering to be the mom rather than the daughter as the queen of family life domain.

1.4—Power as Muscle Mastery (Potty Training) while Being Loved in the Mess

Freud provides a vivid image of pride/mastery vs shame/failure with the adventures of "Captain Underwear" - potty training. As parents, don't you remember those years in the diaper aisle only to return when the next baby comes? Now here they are at almost three still messing their diapers and being able to tell you what to do! What is wrong with this picture? As parents, you probably remember the shame you felt when you made a mess in your underwear as a toddler and you don't want to shame your child. Potty training now takes longer for today's parents, probably with better results than Freud's day for enduring untidy messes which symbolize the mess of our human condition.

To normalize for both you and your child, you read the book that describes how all the animal kingdom "poops": birds poop and it looks like this, bears poop, fish poop, ducks poop and you could tell what animal did what in the snow from the size and shape of their droppings. One version of the anal vision that the family goes through is where there is always the smell of some kind of poop somewhere, if not the baby, then the cat's litter box, or the dog's collection of poop in the yard that hasn't been picked up. This is one experience of the anal side of ordinary life.

Freud has a different vision of the anal stage that relates failures in potty training to distortions in adult personalities "He is so anal" means that a person is too obsessive about neatness but another "anal" distortion is the opposite wherein someone who rebelled against a regime of potty training not to their liking is the opposite of neat - a sloppy mess-maker. Two extremes of potty traumas were represented as Oscar (mess) and Felix (neat) in the film "The Odd Couple" describing the consequences of a mismatch of roommates. Felix can't stand that Oscar leaves the kitchen piled up with dishes and feels compelled to clean up after him, but he draws the line about cleaning Oscar's room piled up with dirty clothes and old food from last night's meal. Yuk! Oscar is easy-going and go-with-the-flow and he sees Felix as uptight and inflexible, "anal", but without seeing himself as a "slob". Felix and Oscar present us with another example of the need for a middle path which incorporates the best of each and leaves out the worst, esp. for roommates or marital mates.

1.5—The Integration of Love (warmth) and Power (authority) in Parenting

Research has found that the most optimal parenting style combines the opposites of warmth or nurturance (love) with the authority of rules and maturity of demands which require communication between child and parent. Diana Baumrind has focused on 4 dimensions of parenting in her attempt to identify what to follow and what to change which is the "Authoritative style". Two other parenting styles are "Authoritarian" and the "Permissive" but both lack something. The Authoritarian has a high level of demand and control but low levels of warmth and communication with the consequence that these children do well in school but have lower self-esteem and are typically less skilled with peers. Some appear subdued while others show high aggressiveness. These traits last well into high school and sometimes beyond.

The Permissive style of parenting is high in warmth and communication but too low in demand and control with the consequence that these children do slightly worse in school during adolescence, are somewhat less mature, less independent, and less likely to take responsibility. Surprisingly, they tend to be more aggressive.

Authoritative parenting that is high in warmth and communication (love) as well as high in demand and control (power) has the most consistently positive outcomes with these children showing higher self-esteem, more independence, more compliance with parental requests, more altruistic behaviors, and more self-confidence with an achievement orientation for better grades in school. The parents tend to be more involved in their child's school work. When discipline is required, the parents explain to the child why a punished behavior is wrong and help the child to regain control of their behavior and gain perspective of other's feelings (empathy). This authoritative parenting style is most frequently found in middle class, educated white families that are intact, but there are good outcomes found for all ethnic groups who practice it. Successful parenting at the start combines secure attachment with authoritative parenting.

1.6—Freudian Love as Possession and Power for Manipulating of Parents

The Oedipal Complex of Freud seems to bring a stretch of preschool sexuality into the realm of immature power manipulation. The preschool child has a different relationship with the mother than he has with the father and likes different parents in different ways based on his needs. At this stage, as the child favors the mom over the dad, he begins to realize that both parents like expressions of his love and approval and therein is a source of power to play one off over the other.

The child may want the mom's nurturing and reject the intrusion of the father who has been out working all day. As a pre-verbal baby this was okay for the father but now the dad wants more interaction with his son. On another day, the child may want to go out into the outside world of his dad, want to learn gender roles, learn tools or play sports and then mom is put on the back burner. The child picks up the mom's feelings around the rejection and discovers power in the family triad.

Freud made a great deal of this stage believing that the unfulfilled desires and fantasies of this stage led to women wanting an older father figure upon whom they would "transfer" their repressed childhood longings. The high level of sexual repression during the Victorian period in Austria led to a great need to work through sexual dreams and fantasies causing unconscious motivations for irrational behavior and abnormal ("perverted") sexual behavior

By the time of preschool, usually another competitor has arrived on the scene in the form of a new baby to "dethrone" the only child from being the center of attention. Freud left this topic to his disciple Alfred Adler who saw power as a major component in different kinds of competition between siblings in the family. Remember the "Smothers Brothers" routine of "Mom always loved you best"?

1.7—The Power Complexes of Superiority and Inferiority Complexes

According to Erik Erikson, the roots of inferiority may develop during this second toddler stage of activity if there is a lack of physical fitness or athletic deficiency but shame is more likely to develop in a competitive context of "the family constellation". Alfred Adler saw power as a more dominant motivator than love arising with the "sibling rivalry" that develops when the first born child is "dethroned" from central stage as the only child by the birth of a second child.

The baby needs more attention than the older first born and is loved just for being the newborn baby. The older child tries to win the parents' attention back by achievements or misdeeds (power) but the baby is still in the center stage just for little smiles and needing hugs (love).

The main power play in the family becomes the first born's determination to prove that he is superior and powerful and that the last born is weak and inferior. In Chapter five, Adler tells his story of battling inferiority first with an older brother with a superiority complex and then with his mentor Freud who also insisted on staying number one without compromise. Adler sketches a number of combinations of character types with one person dominant over the other which allows for a bridge into the nine Enneagram character types contrasting the leader/follower types in chapter six.

Three of the Enneagram types are motivated by the power of superiority: the Perfectionist (#1), the Achiever (#3) and the Asserter (#8). Three other Enneagram types are willing to offer non-competitive connection (love) rather than being in a conflictual relationship. These three types are the Helper (#2), the Peacemaker (#9), and one who is loyal until doubt brings change (#6 the Loyal Skeptic). Three others chose to seek love and/or power from within themselves first before interacting in any competitive format: the Adventurer (#7) seeks fun (love of life), the Romantic cultivates creativity (#4) and the Observer (#5) needs a distance to prepare for interaction with control.

While the attachment theory (via Freud) focuses specifically on marriage relationships, the Enneagram contrasts (via Adler) can be seen as power conflicts in the work place, among family members, and with couples. Adler's main theory of sibling rivalry also shows up in all settings but with some surprises. One would expect the first born to dominate and the later born to fight this domination. When a first born sister gets along with a later born brother, it is expected that marrying a later born husband who gets along with his first born sister will work out with more love than conflict. Furthermore, middle born children are often outside of the first born ruler and last born baby scenario by avoiding both extreme roles to find a middle path of their own making.

Just as each stage of life has an overriding goal, so does each character type have a passion to answer the existential question: What is the purpose and meaning of my life? The Perfectionist wants to achieve the ideal of rightness, the Achiever wants success, the Asserter wants control, the Helper wants to meet the needs of others to feel loved, the Pleaser want to agree with others to feel close, and the Loyalist feels loved when aligned with approving authority figures. Adventurers live to have fun, Romantics live to be creative, and Observers want independence and autonomy from anyone trying to control them.

1.8—Power as Superiority in School and Love as Peer Closeness

With full time elementary school, the family dramas take the back stage, transferred to the school setting in downsized forms, but the self-directed pursuit of competence and academic achievements is where the energy goes in what Freud calls the Latency (non-sexual stage) where closeness is with same sex friends with some emotional distance from parents through the separation caused by school with teachers as parent substitutes and unrelated classmates as sib substitutes.

Elementary school is a long period of learning competence in academics and extracurricular skills (sports, music, drama) either for superiority or inferiority. Connection and support by the parents lead to an easy, familiar intimacy of closeness with little drama. Happiness for the elementary school child is experiencing mastery and success among peers in the major academic subjects and the most important group skill development activities with a performance and rating side: sports and/or the arts.

The competition for grades and success in sports is the setting ripe for the sibling rivalry of the family to emerge with different unrelated players acting out the one-up or one-down roles of the sibling scripts. I recall both the benefits of a first born friend acting in the role of a big brother helping me with sports and Boy Scouts. I also recall the pain of inferiority as he made a point of his superiority in sports and math. In fifth grade, our seats were arranged by our Friday test scores in math so everyone could see that my superior friend is tops in the "A" row while I was embarrassingly somewhere in the back too close to the bullies. Our report cards gave us clear feedback as to how we were succeeding in our mastery of academics (as well as sports and the arts) to either give us hope or concern about our futures. Since the high profile pecking order was math, science and sports, I was surprised to find myself on a college track by the end of elementary school with the social sciences, history and other humanities. I was also surprised that the humility that I learned through my shortcomings was more appreciated by the other gender than the bragging of my superior friend which helped my self-esteem (even though I didn't understand it). Sometimes accepting smallness was a truth with benefits.

1.9—The Teen Identity Crisis of Both Power and Love

The stable identity and closeness with parents of these first 8 years of school become unstable during the teen period with major growth spurts and hormonal changes. Teens become less close to parents through some form of separation or independence from parental guidance replaced by the influence of peers and the media. Teens are intensely attracted to the opposite gender for intimacy needs but nothing but physical intimacy is possible without a stable identity and closeness. Without the needed boundaries, closeness becomes the anxious "fusion" of two people who don't know their identities. The big question is "who am I?" The "individuation" process of separating from parental values and dependencies and replacing both with the teen's own values and provision is a deep level of empowerment. The anxiety of a missing identity drives teens to identify and conform to the values and norms of their peer groups which often contrast with parental standards. The task for the teen period is to find an integrated identity during an "identity crisis" or stay for a prolonged period with a fragmented, conflicted identity lacking integration. Adults find it ironic that teens are rebelling in such similar ways with their dress, hair-dos and speech that they end up conforming to the peer group without knowing any better their unique identities.

Teens are impatient with their reliance upon their parents for rent, car and basics when they are critical of their parents who seem to want to control them too much and snoop on their parties with friends. Teens are often embarrassed of their parents before their peer groups because parents seem old fashioned, retro, not cool, and they would prefer to be driving, eating and entertaining with friends rather than their parents who own the car and pay their expenses.

One parent with a sense of humor put up this sign for his teenagers:

> *"TEENS, ARE YOU TIRED OF BEING DEPENDENT ON YOUR STUPID PARENTS? WHY NOT MOVE OUT TO MAKE YOUR <u>OWN</u> LIVING TO SHOW US HOW SMART YOU ARE."*

Teens do better when they are able to avoid a broken relationship with their parents and agree to disagree in tolerable ways while keeping affection (intimacy) for each other. The locomotion empowerment of a license and use of the family car increases self-esteem and confidence in dating the opposite gender.

Sexuality is a big preoccupation for teens and Freud (and his followers) have much to say on this topic. The discovery of the new biology based on Darwin's evolutionary theory was a revolution for Freud who saw the Puritanical Victorian culture of his time as cut off from the biological power of sexual "polymorphous perverse" passions as the cause of repressed hidden secrets that divided the soul bringing on physical and mental suffering. What Freud discovered continues to be foundational in psychology but with the balancing modifications of his early and later followers. Did you really want to have sex with your mother and kill your father? Is the pursuit of the deepest possible sexual satisfactions really a true basis for a new religion as it is mixed with drug states and crossing every line? For all his contributions the popularization of Freud's idea of freedom from all sexual repression is a ticket for developmental deformity if we follow the criticism of the Neo-Freudian Eric Fromm. Our basic institution of the family is rooted in the moral heroism of marital fidelity despite whatever"polymorphous" fantasies we may have in the temptations which sees the forbidden as somehow the most desirable.

Finally the teens do leave home for college, receive training for a career and find sufficient employment to support themselves. This first goal of empowered autonomy allows for the second goal of building intimacy as a couple so that dependence and independence can be merged into interdependence.

Leaving home for college is a big step toward autonomy, but college students are still in the "betwixt and between" of teenagers where they are more "preparing for work" than filling the adult career slot. Students work part-time jobs, get money from their parents as well as loans and/or scholarships but are not self-sufficient and are often poor like the characters in the Opera "La Boheme" who do art, poetry and philosophy but can hardly pay the rent.

Neither are male students able to take on a spouse or a child and the best they can do is "play house" with a girl friend without any lasting commitment. When I ask students in my classes to make a stair case of goals leading to what they consider "happiness", they invariably list getting the BA (and MA if needed) so they get a career job with sufficient money, wait until their mate has their career in hand, get married, get a good house in a good school district and have 2.5 kids.

As I follow them up years later, this is what they tend to do with some getting married soon after the BA and doing jobs outside of their ideal career track. They felt like adults to hold a full time job, live away from parents, and be self-supportive on the salaries of the two couples albeit with big college debts to carry for years

1.10—An Overview of Heroism in the First Five "Crises" of Life

The concept of **heroism** *may be seen through Erik Erikson's observation in each of pre-adult stages that the pursuit of fulfillment (happiness) involves* **facing a crisis** *in the transition from one stage to the next. This crisis involves various kinds of unhappiness (discomfort, conflict, confusion) until an adjustment resolution is developed. The outcome may be a peak of success or a pit of failure. The infant gains trust (for intimacy) and the toddler achieves autonomy (for empowerment). Failing to reach these landmarks of growth in a timely way brings the infant into the pits of mistrust, insecurity, and the toddler into self-doubt and shame.*

Instinctually we are programmed to pursue what is pleasurable and to avoid or flee from pain for basic survival. Facing the discomfort of each crisis point of change with courage, effort and persistence takes us into the realm of "heroism". We face our fears and our resistance to change (complacency, inertia) and make the breakthrough into a new domain. Through each crisis, we gain some virtue of moral heroism: trust, autonomy, will power, creative planning, competence, integrated identity, intimacy, mentoring, wisdom and life acceptance.

CHAPTER TWO

SEEKING HAPPINESS THROUGH ADULT POWER AND LOVE

2.1—The "Good Fit" Search for Stable Happiness in Marriage

We now transition to the adult love/family topography of the last three stages of the lifespan wherein secure attachment leads to the peak in the intimacy of married love for young adults and then is continued through midlife with the need for caring for two generations: adult children and aging parents.

The sages of all ages have sung the praises of a lasting happiness as a treasure to be sought in the right places. The lifespan tasks show a continual movement pulled by short and long term goals of happiness such as finding a successful career and marriage.

The first clue for success in both the power of work and the intimacy of love is stability. The inevitable "pits" of our "human condition" require us to develop the art of resilience so that we might return from the pits of despair or grief unto the more stable middle path. The happiness research shows that there are both stable and unstable sources of happiness. A prudent beginning of our journey (led by adult choices) would be to find the most stable and lasting forms of happiness as that fulfilled sense of subjective wellbeing.

The contrast between the unstable "feel good happiness" and the more stable "good fit" happiness in the research of Martin Seligman provides the second clue that stability is related to finding a "good fit" in two major time investments in our life: our marriage/family and work/career.

According to studies by Seligman (2000 and 2002) married people are happier than any other configuration with 40% of marrieds saying that they were "very happy" in contrast to 24% of those living together, 22% of those never married, and 18% of those previously married (divorced). The research suggests that the wellbeing (happiness) of adults continues to increase over time despite the changes from the peaks of honeymoon period in and out of the pits of seeing the idealized other as a normal, sometimes annoying earthling like ourselves.

The difference between the happy and unhappy couples seems to swing on two parts of communication: the ability to resolve conflicts with flexibility and the ability of communication to build on personal compatibility and trust into greater closeness. Communication skills help partners work through problems and pursue both a breadth and depth of knowledge about each other leading to the peak fulfillment of intimacy wherein our true selves are revealed with minimal defenses and optimal transparency. Thus 75% of the happy couples cited the intimate quality of their communication which was present in only 11% of the unhappy couples. (Seligman in Williams text, p7) The communication issues include a breadth of topics from expressions of love/sexuality through money management and the highest values of spirituality as well as discovering religious, political and personality differences. Finding recurrent intimacy in a lasting marriage appears to be one source of a stable happiness capable of lasting most or all of one's lifetime. Along with the "good fit" in marriage compatibility, the skills and virtues of "marriage fitness" are required for success.

The fruit of the seeds of the love connection and striving for independence is yielded in the young and mid-life stages of marriage and career in adulthood. The vacillation between dependence and independence of early childhood becomes an integration of the two poles in the interdependent mutuality of marriage. Each partner takes a turn of being a dependent recipient of some service kindness in the reciprocity of marriage which moves the couple into greater intimacy of mutual sharing and closeness with gender differences. Women move into deeper communication and conflict resolution activities quickly and with apparent satisfaction while men tend to need persuasion and lessons in both. What makes the difference between successful and struggling marriages?

2.2—The Need for the "Heroism of Fitness to Sustain "Good Fit"

We are warned that falling in love" of the honeymoon stage needs another more mature stage of "standing in love" according to Eric Fromm in his classic book "The Art of Loving (1956). Fromm envisions marital love as an "art" that must be taught to balance the illusory peak of "falling in love". Only through developing one's total personality do we gain capacity of loving one's spouse with **"true humility, courage, faith and discipline"**. (Fromm, pp.110 & 120) Without developing these virtues of "moral heroism", the illusory peak will be followed by a pit of falling out of love.

The initial attraction of a dating couple is for an increase of pleasure and wellbeing but true love will require a foregoing of one's own pleasure to promote of the "beloved other" moving from the "I-it" relationship of using a woman's body as a sex object to the "I-Thou" relationship of loving the other as a full person as intrinsically valuable as oneself. (Martin Buber's "**I and Thou**"). The early sacrifices that loving couples do willingly driven by the love foreshadow the later sacrifices of caring for dependent children (and later dependent aged parents).

Marriage is not for "sissies" or the immature but is the symbolic initiation into adulthood which will require the maturity to rise above one's own selfish needs for the larger good of providing for family (and extended family) needs.

Fromm's focus on the virtues of humility, faith, courage, and submission to discipline also belong to another level of "I-Thou" relationship of man's love of God as seen in the numerous awesome cathedrals all over Europe. Man's passion for union with his ultimate Source is not limited to the institutions of religion but spiritual fitness values are most coherently articulated in various sacred texts and mystical phenomena,

2.3—The Realistic Embrace of Both the Peaks and Pits of Marriages

Successful marriages are built on realistic expectations of marriage where the peaks are connected to growing through hard times.

Realistically it can be expected that two like-minded, compatible people who share everything as a couple in marriage will **double their joys and their caring support for each other.**

It can also be predicted that two individuals with differences in gender, personality. and baggage from their families of origin will inevitably **double the sorrows and the burdens** for each other. If each partner can commit to both the peak and pits sides of this marriage equation, the couple will come to realize that marriage is an heroic joint pursuit of happiness. In the marriage vows, couples will affirm that they are banking their future fulfillment not only on their "good fit" as a compatible couple but upon their willingness to grow in "spiritual fitness" as their characters are challenged to meet both peaks and pits with resilience to be "transformed by trouble" (Rick Warren's "Purpose-Driven Life").

Those with realistic expectations will not be disappointed with the inevitable challenges. Strengths are used to compensate for weaknesses. Weaknesses are reframed as growth opportunities allowing the focus to avoid being problem centered while still addressing relationship challenges. In this way a a realistic map of the marriage territory may be found as the pursuit of happiness takes the form of "moral heroism" in order to grow both from the pits of sorrows/burdens as well as the peaks of marriage support and joys.

The core essence of marriage includes balanced reciprocity or the mutuality of the give and take over time. There should be a positive net gain when costs are subtracted from benefits for each partner. If one partner continually gets a negative net loss with this "social exchange" equation, the inequality becomes a source of imbalance and injustice. The combination of one partner's selfishness and the codependency of the other partner can perpetuate a marriage misfit. A new set of virtues (spiritual fitness) need to be attained for justice, forgiveness and healing. Working through a difficult partnership or ending it to find a new marriage are different forms of heroism hopefully before a full marriage with children. Both decisions require the virtues of "humility, *courage, faith and discipline" as Fromm directs. Ideally, both partners in the marriage are striving to become their best selves and not exploiting the goodness of the other.*

2.4—Secure and Insecure Attachment in Adult Relationships

The teen time is a challenge for self-love as well as the power of separating from the love dependency on parents, the connection love to peers and the immature infatuation with members of the opposite gender (a quasi-love).

As we look over the adult stages of the lifespan we see the dualistic dance of two opposing drives becoming coordinated into a unified whole with a couple who procreate individuals who are raised, eventually launched and who eventually become their own couple combination gifting their parents with the joy of being grandparents. The choreography of life moves from opposition into wholeness only to be transformed by more challenges in power and love.

As we look at the changes in both power and love in the family cycle from young adults to seniors, fluctuations in the level of happiness (as wellbeing) can be seen in gains and losses.

As an adult, the securely connected adult has a wide range of emotions and expresses them well in expressing needs, asking of help or hearing the needs of other and providing for help. They have the good boundaries of assertions to say "no" to others even when others protest. They can be confrontative (power) but they also know how to play and have fun (love of life). Securely attached adults have the right "self love" which allows them to accept both their weaknesses and those of others. They can describe strengths and weakness in themselves and others without idealizing or devaluating. They are able to handle conflict, negative emotions, and give room for others to disagree. Secure Connectors promote reciprocity and balanced giving in relationships. They do not feel uncomfortable with new situations, can take risks, and can delay gratification. They feel comfortable with intimacy (love) as well as independence and can balance the two (integration).

The nature of attachment (secure or insecure) is foundational so that everything built from that point is either on a strong or weak foundation but still continues on through the stages with problems arising when resolutions have been lacking. Attachment theory is a Neo-Freudian adaptation of Freud that is more amenable to research with good, consistent results. Freud thought that the major motivation of humans was for body-based love and the major unhappiness was due to repression of this basic drive due to culturally restrictive norms which keep the infant from unhurried breast feeding and skin contact with the mother.

Contrast this capacity of the securely connected adult with marital breakdowns discussed under Freudian attachment theory in chapter five such as the Vacillator/Avoider combination or the Controller/Victim mismatch. The first has a mismatch of too much emotional need combined with someone who has too little tolerance for emotions. The second mismatch has one person (the Controller) with too much power connected to someone with too little power (Victim or could be the Pleaser). Love and power are not balanced or integrated in any of these combinations so as to lack the essential mutuality and reciprocity essential to marriage. (see ch. 5, 5.3).

2.5—The Heroism Needed for the Peaks and Pits of Parenting

Details of the love (caregiving) and power (discipline) required in parenting will be seen in the parenting landscape but one peak and pit that stands out as major challenges come from having the first baby. The illusory peaks of idealistic expectations about motherhood set up the stressful pits of the unexpected chaos and loss of sleep when the newborn enters the parents' world.

Betty Carter in her study of parenting, concludes that once there is a child"life will never be the same again, for better (peaks) **and** for worse (pits)." Carter describes the early months of having a newborn as a "shock" to new parents with many challenges ranging from "sleep deprivation, shredded schedules, endless chores" to worrying about the baby's development and one's own competence feeling a need for "ceaseless vigilance." (Carter, p. 249) "No amount of doing ever seems enough to get the job done before it needs to be done again" and so the threat of chaos "puts enormous stress on new parents and on their relationship". (Ibid.) These pits are more than matched by the fact that most parents "fall passionately in love with their new babies and consider them fascinating, delightful and unique additions to the family." (Ibid.)

Singles who saw the costs of parenting seeming to outweigh the benefits asked a support group of new parents: "Why does anyone have children? It's too hard!" Carter then described the unanimous, spontaneous response from the parents as they began to "laugh in astonishment" and begin to almost "fall all over each other" as they described the joys, the pleasures, and the transcendence of parenthood while admitting that it was almost impossible to put into words the physical, sensory, intellectual, emotional, and spiritual experience of connectedness to another human being through the kind of tangible, selfless love, inspired by caring for their young children. (Car, 271) Carter herself has never met any adult who regretted becoming a parent despite the obvious challenges and pits int today's world.

Looking at the natural peaks (ups) and pits (downs) in the family cycle provides an additional perspective in the context of the current happiness research.

The capacity of love to sacrifice happiness for the greater good is an heroic power that brings resilience to family happiness during hard times. Love becomes a power to sustain loss with positivity to balance a one-track duality of happiness (or unhappiness) with a joy in the midst of a loss that has been accepted, heroically.

When a couple become parents, they limit their capacity to nurture each other for two decades of child rearing but the "empty nest" of midlife brings a restoration of this quality time for the couples. The new challenges of high rents, high college costs, low job availability lead to temporary couples who break up or temporary jobs with launched young adults returning home or becoming an ongoing source of worry at a distance. The parents of mid- lifers lose a spouse, lose independent functioning and move into the midlife empty nest for caregiving. For the midlife couple, power has meant autonomy while love has meant the sacrifice of that autonomy to give the familiar love of caregiving now to a parent to complete another cycle.

Each stage at the adult level has both a positive reward when developmental goals are achieved and a negative consequence when these goals are failed to be reached. The same is true of the pre-adult stages. Our interest in the pre-adult stages is to see the source of either success or challenges in power or love. The three founding fathers of psychology (Freud, Adler and Jung) discovered the profound impact of the early childhood on later life as to love attachment (Freud), power competition (Adler) or the need to integrate and reconcile the opposition of power and love. Jung cites moral heroism (character virtues) of Biblical and folk heroes who show that the power of love can be stronger than the love of power with paradoxes against the odds so that the last might become first and the first last. The Enneagram is one perspective on the range of character types present in our human family and **all** have some mix of virtues (detachment from distortions in either power or love) and vices (addictions to either domination or compromise to avoid conflict). The love given by family for secure attachment as well as the empowerment to separate for our own autonomy provide the raw material for the moral heroism needed for the pursuit of happiness throughout the entire lifespan journey. We also need first hand examples of living heroes who demonstrate the power of our higher self to overcome the addictions and negativity of our lower self.

In the above example, we see the parental loss of power (control) with the birth of a new baby as well as a new view of love as "tangible, selfless, caring for children" which allow parents to celebrate both the pits (sacrifices) and peaks (joys) of parenting. A new concept of love emerges which connects the opposites of married parents with celibate nuns and monks - self sacrificing service for a transcendent love. If we seek the essence and integrating core of love, this aspect might be close.

The couple finds intimacy through both the thunder showers and the sunshine of their emotional life together. The wholeness of intimacy requires both fair fighting and emotional closeness, the power of conflict resolution and the empathy of communication. As the couple become a family, they become connected to their urban community for daycare, school, churches, sports, clubs that foster talents and special interests.

2.6—The Spiritual Fitness to Love and Work in Family Life

Although mutuality is an ideal of marriage, the caring for children will involve a one-sided giving of finances, effort, time, and love that may never be returned. Social psychologists claim that we are genetically hard wired to reproduce the human species. The years of pregnancy are limited in time causing a woman to feel her "biological clock ticking" with an urgency to become pregnant and thus fulfill the inbuilt role of her womb and hormones to create a new life. Children generally outlive their parents and thus give an extended life to the family and clan as a kind of natural transcendence of their mortality. Since children are not clones, their unique identities may contrast sharply with the careers, lifestyles and spiritual values of their parents who must give both roots (secure attachment) as well as wings (freedom to be oneself).

The high costs of rent in urban areas combined with high college tuition and low availability of the right fit entry jobs make launching into full independence difficult for this new generation of young adults extending the need for midlife parents to provide economic support. The care and/or concern for children can go on for decades and then comes the midlife caring for their aging parents. The work of family is made easier by the quality of genuine love and made harder by unresolved conflicts or lack of real connection. For most parents, there are seasons of intense engagement followed by other seasons of relative freedom from daily obligations.

Children can be quite impacted by the peaks of parental love memories and the pits of parental mistakes. Becoming parents themselves, helps young adults understand and forgive the honest mistakes of their parents. A divorce or death of a parent at a critical developmental time for a child may take some years to forgive, heal, move on. Guilt is often a complication to working through a normal grief over family losses. Having a religious faith can be a help in grieving, forgiveness and the release of guilt.

2.7—Power and Love at Midlife with Adult Children

The raising of a family requires both competence and relational skills gained from the earlier stages and is a very busy time where the partners may lose track of who they were in their original relationship. Suddenly the kids are launched off to college and/or independent lives and the midlife crisis of the rediscovering intimacy between the couples can happy with a sudden awareness of one's mortality. The "empty nest" can be an opportunity to rediscover each other or a shocking discovery that your co-worker in parenting is a stranger. Is that why God created grandchildren? A chance for a new beginning with a new generation, a new lease on feeling young again (or more worn out) but new life challenges with both peaks and potential pits. One virtue of caring is acquired during this stage and given to both aging parents and young grandchildren.

The early senior years can be a continuation of the midlife peaks and pits with the pits of one's mortality coming in waves. During midlife, parents were taking care of their own parents in declining health but the early age seniors are having to face the pits of the dying and deaths of their own parents. Death becomes real, can be tragic, feels like absolute loss, and the pits of grief follow. This early senior stage (65-75) could also witness breakdowns in the launching of their children through unemployment and/or divorce requiring caring support. More difficult still for this age group, may be the need to care for the medical needs of one's spouse as one walks through a mine field of illnesses to which seniors are vulnerable such as heart attacks, cancer, diabetes, surgeries for knees and/or hips. The love capability developed throughout marriage is taken to a higher level of willing sacrifice which is surprise peak of fulfillment as love grows deeper, more tangible, more authentic.

2.8—Power and Love for Oldest Seniors during Peaks and Pits

According to Erikson the challenge of the last stage of seniors is between "ego integrity" (the sense that one has lived a useful life) vs hopelessness where one's life by the end is not acceptable. Older adults become more reflective and philosophical and those who do become less fearful of death. Seeing old age in terms of variability rather than universal decline can help seniors accept this stage better as some reap the benefits of healthy choices made earlier in life and respond to health crises in positive ways to makes positive differences in aging. Elders who help others and remain active in a community (love connections) exhibit higher levels of physical and emotional functioning and productivity through becoming volunteers, they perform unpaid work for altruistic reasons. Having new pursuits offers productivity options such as taking music lessons or attending college classes. Some report staying healthier by being active in art classes.

The positive variability in aging is known as the "Successful Aging Paradigm" showing that senior can have happiness despite natural physical losses.

The "use it or lose it" principle applies to cognitive abilities as seniors who remain engaged in cognitively-challenging environments are able to minimize loses in thinking and learning abilities. Staying actively engaged in life with ongoing learning combined with sufficient physical fitness (diet and exercise) are keys to successful aging again showing the combination of virtues to the continued pursuit of happiness.

The cumulative lessons of successful coping with stressors help elders cope better with stress than young adults due to more life experiences. Older adults tend to accept the limits of their power with age and instead try to manage their stress related emotional response. Those elders who managed internal control over important life "domains" with personally relevant, normal activities were able to age well.(Ibid.)

Having a sense of control (power) is essential to a sense of personal well-being (happiness). Financial decisions may not cause stress if the individual feels in control. Perception of control matters as much as actual control. Social comparisons facilitate feelings of control.

When it comes to living Arrangements, most elders prefer the empowerment and intimate familiarity of "aging in place" by making modifications to a private residence. Changing a normal environment is much preferable to moving into an institution. Comprehensive home-based care has strong positive effects on elder's physical and mental health (empowerment and sense of wellbeing). Elders age best when their social networks remain stable with some close relationships. Adaptations are necessary with the death of significant relatives but it is possible to replace previous missing ties through volunteer activities and interest groups.

There is a tendency for elders to seek spiritual intimacy in times of stress which may be important in later life when there is a higher number of life stressors Elders who place high emphasis on religious faith tend to worry much less. Associations between religious faith and physical and mental health have been found among diverse faiths. Faith has positive effects associated with how elders think about their lives and provides elders with a positive theme to integrate various periods of life (spiritual empowerment) Religious service attendance can provide a social aspect necessary for improved health. Individuals who attend church are more likely to comply with medical advice. The virtues of moral heroism are particularly needed to reframe death from failure into graduation. (See #14, Boyd text, on "Seniors")

CHAPTER THREE

PEAKS AND PITS IN POWER AND LOVE AS WE DIE

"Can you tell me, boss...why do people die?"

"I don't know, Zorba," I replied, ashamed, as If I had been asked the simplest, the most essential thing, and was unable to explain it.

"You don't know! Well all those damned books you read- what good are they? Why do you read them if they don't tell you that, what do they tell you?...I want you to tell me where we come from and where we are going to?"

...I felt deep within me that the highest point a man can attain is...something more heroic and more despairing: Sacred Awe!" (N. Kazantzakis, p.300)

3.1—Power and Love in the Face of a Tragic Death

When a young friend dies prematurely from violence or serious illness that could be avoided, we experience the anguish, grief and confusion described by Zorba and seek a wider source of transcendent meaning of life: "where do we come from and where are we going to?" What good are all the "damned books" if they don't try to answer this *question? Zorba's intellectual comrade felt a "sacred awe" that was both heroic and despairing in realizing that the answer was beyond his capability as a man to do more than share the pain of sorrow and meaninglessness with compassion and presence. Zorba sought comfort facing the vastness of the sea while he danced until he fell down from exhaustion with both tears and anger. Death seems to bring an ultimate loss of meaning and purpose to life. We seek something more ultimate than death for which the endlessness of the sea symbolizes toward which our "sacred awe" moves us: a secure attachment to our Author and Finisher. What if our loss has been the tangible source of our secure attachment such as a spouse or a parent? How can an invisible, sometimes faraway God make up the difference?*

The answer of "how we die" can be answered by science but "why we die" belongs to the realm of philosophy/religion. This chapter examines what science knows about the process of dying before, during and after in the grief afterwards for survivors. Religious wisdom traditions for centuries have described a time of exceptional power and love which contemporary Near Death Experiences tend to confirm despite the challenge to the empirical only paradigms of traditional science. We begin with the question of how we die and how we recover from the loss of our secure attachment to a beloved friend or relative.

3.2—The Destruction of the Physical Body after Death

Death was once defined as the cessation of the heartbeat and of breathing, but breathing and heartbeat can sometimes be restarted through CPR and life support devices such as pace makers. "Brain death" or "biological death" are used today to define a person as being dead. The empirical evidence of death is that brain activity stops which is clinical death. Brain death is when the person no longer has reflexes or any response to vigorous external stimuli. Brain death is the complete and irreversible loss of brain function necessary to sustain life.

Immediately after the heart stops beating, the body rapidly cools down until it reaches room temperature ("Algor Mortis"). Without the heart pumping, blood coagulates in the veins, arteries and capillaries, causing the entire body to stiffen. "Rigor mortis" sets in around two to six hours after death. A few days after death, bacteria begin to break down the body until finally one month after death the organs are liquified leaving nothing lasting but the skeleton. (Ashitha Nagesh for Metro.co.uk 9/28/15)

3.3—Experiences of Love and Empowerment After Death in NDE's

Normally the part of the brain which controls thoughts and emotions is shut down into a coma before dying but one patient was in a coma for seven days but able to be revived. This patient was a neurosurgeon who describes his dying as follows.

"E. coli bacteria had penetrated my cerebrospinal fluid, were eating my brain, my chances of survival in anything beyond a vegetative state went from low to nothing. For seven days I lay in a deep coma with my higher-order brain functions "totally offline" but just as the doctors were deciding whether to discontinue treatment, "my eyes popped open". While the neurosurgeon had been in a coma, he discovered a consciousness (that) exists beyond the body. (Alexander in Newsweek, 2008) What the neurosurgeon observed fits better with religion than science.

Above the clouds, I saw "flocks of transparent, shimmering beings arced across the sky" which he considered "advanced, higher forms of being" who were "content and overjoyed" giving a "glorious chant" as they moved. "Everything was distinct, yet everything was also a part of everything else, like the rich and intermingled designs on a Persian carpet... or a butterfly's wing." The experience just described fits into the phenomenon known as NDE - Near Death Experiences of a round trip beyond death and back.

3.4—Patterns of After Life Experiences based on NDE Data

*According to the Out-Of-Body Experience Research Center in Los Angeles, more than **8 million** Americans have reported NDEs, which occur when a person is either clinically dead, near dead or in a situation where death is likely or expected.*

Many people who have had near-death experiences report similar sensations: feeling as though they were floating outside of their bodies, moving rapidly through a tunnel toward light or seeing deceased loved ones.

One of the earliest and most complete account of what happens after physical death is a study by a medical doctor, Raymond Moody. Dr. Moody studied 150 cases of NDE (near death experiences) and found recurrent patterns with some variations.

So what is it like to die according to Dr. Moody? The dying person is in crisis but just as person reaches the point of greatest physical distress, a loud buzzing is heard as the individual moves through a long dark tunnel rapidly to find oneself outside of one's physical body and able to see the person's dead body from above with some state of emotional upheaval. The deceased person finds himself in a different kind of body but soon adjusts to this odd condition and begins to see relatives and friends who have already died.

Soon a "being of light" appears asking the deceased nonverbally to evaluate the life just completed seen as a panoramic, instantaneous playback of every major event of the person's life. This being of light is nonjudgmental and very loving helping the reviewed life to be accepted with its imperfections. A border between earthly life and the afterlife appears but the individual cannot yet pass over because it is not yet time but must return to complete life on earth. The out of body person does not want to return to earth because of such intense feelings of joy, love and peace in this realm but suddenly the spiritual body is reunited with the physical body for life to continue. Re-entry into the body is painful because of its serious near death state, but the person no longer fears death and continues to cherish this ineffable experience. Most people are skeptical of the NDE shared and there is some difficulty adjusting to a life so much less perfect than the one outside the body. (Moody, p.22-23).

In general, being in a spiritual body is free of pain and fear but there is some distress that no one living can hear them as they try to get help and no one can see them. This new body can move through solid objects like trees but one's. hands are unable to grasp anything tangible in this world. This new body is weightless allowing the person to rise up in the air and float.

This description also is consistent with the appearance of Christ after his resurrection coming into the room without opening any doors and suddenly disappearing into space. The difference is that Christ's disciples could see and hear him (and even touch him) because his spiritual body was reunited with his physical body but without the limitations of the physical realm.

Quite a few of the NDE persons connect this loving "being of light" with Christ even though there is a spectrum of belief systems represented in the 150 people. The "being of light" was a personal being with a very definite personality with a love and warmth that were utterly beyond words. The newly dead person reports being completely accepted by this person and feels an "irresistible magnetic attraction",drawn to this person of light. The most common identification through all faiths is that this was a "being of light" capable of an unimpeded communication without words with the feeling that the person was understood perfectly. A question posed was about the meaning and sufficiency of the life they had led to that point realizing now that this was the end of it all. "Are you ready to die?" Here's your life lived as a whole, was it "worth it"?

Judging one's life as a whole a hard issue to face but witnesses agreed that the evaluation was free of condemnation, accusations or threats of consequences in the presence of the total love and acceptance of this "being of light". (Moody, 61) The purpose of the question was intended to help the person into better insight and truth about themselves. Since all the people of this study returned to life, the insights would help them live with greater meaning and purpose in the future. What was most life changing was the impact of this all loving spiritual person.

One person dying from a ruptured appendix felt her "real being" come out of her body to encounter this light with a question and implication. "Lovest thou me?" "If you do love me, go back and complete what you began in your life." The dying person noted that "all during this time I felt as though I were surrounded by an overwhelming love and compassion - perfect understanding and perfect love." (63)

Another NDE person described the person of the light as "a fun person" and someone with a definite sense of humor echoed in a more detailed testimony of a soldier who had died in a war.

George Ritchie experienced the "being of light's" humor from his own NDE afterlife as a soldier during WW II. "This brightness seemed to vibrate and shimmer with a kind of holy laughter, not at me and my silliness, but a mirth that seemed to say ...that joy was more lasting still despite all the error and tragedy (of life)." (Ritchie, 72) Ritchie describes a special kind of knowing that was "immediate and complete - a stupendous certainty." What he knew was that **this person was "power itself,** older than time and yet modern... but far more even than power was **"an astonishing love**, a love beyond my wildest imaginings" because this love knew every unlovable thing about Ritchie and yet accepted him with **an unconditional love** just the same. (R. 73) The question that "hung in the dazzling air" for Ritchie was: "**How much have you loved with your life?**" (Ibid)

Outside of the body is **a place of ineffable peace, joy and love** in stark contrast to the turmoil, sadness and destruction of the physical body occurring at this same moment. What lesson for living might one derive from this paradoxical data? Would we fear death and possible tragedies less and trust more in a transcendent goodness? The recurrent admonition of Christ in the New Testament is "Fear not for I am with you even unto the end." (Max Lucado). God's love is greater than our mistakes and we have a competent shepherd for all seasons, all landscapes, even through the lonesome valley of the shadow of death.

Christians do believe that "out of the body, in God's presence" but their concern about the NDE data is that it appears that God's love and redemption is given to everyone. Do we not suffer the consequences of our sins and have later to face a final judgment? Is this depiction of the afterlife an imbalanced "sloppy agape" without marking the consequences of serious sin? Some believing Christians have had a round trip tour of what appears as a place of suffering to balance off the overly optimistic view of the afterlife more in keeping with Biblical theology and less like the new age naive belief that everyone has a good afterlife. Most religions hold that the afterlife is where justice is achieved where it was forfeited on earth.

Non-theistic scientists are shocked that Moody as a doctor would believe that an individual can have consciousness when their brain is a flat-liner non-functional. They try to explain away the phenomenon as drug induced or the compensations of the brain in crisis. Their materialistic paradigm will not allow them to accept another non-material plane of consciousness as advocated by all the religions of the world since time began - a belief in an immortal soul. Moody (and others) have refuted the major challenges such as drug induced, lucid dreaming, confirming what was already believed. In the recent film, "Heaven is for Real", the child had experiences in heaven that were never taught and could report conversations held in various rooms while he was in a brain-dead flat liner.

At least three surprises remain. How could there be such freedom from pain outside the body when the physical body is in crisis re-experienced upon the return? How does someone pronounced dead feel at peace so quickly with little adjustment to such a dramatic change? How could there be so much continuity between everyday life and these out of body experiences? Most of those having NDE's were not different than the rest of us in thinking that physical death meant the end of everything. One woman said, "I wasn't sorry that I was dead but I just couldn't figure out where I was supposed to go. My thoughts and my consciousness were just like they were in life." (M, 42)

If we could live fully persuaded of God's complete, perfect and unchanging love for us, we would live with less anxiety and judgments against ourselves and others. At first many survivors of NDE's are depressed and disappointed that they cannot be in the ideal world they experienced but eventually they accept their life as it is and are inspired to make the rest of their life meaningful while accepting death as a reward at the end.

What appears as our last act in the body becoming a skeleton provides motivation to believe in the 8,000 plus NDE reports of the soul (good ghost) moving out of the body before it self-destructs and finding a new spiritual community of love and power. The great contrast between physical appearance and spiritual reality is described in the Book of Wisdom (3:1-9). The choice for virtue is rewarded.

> "The souls of the virtuous are in God's hands and no torment shall ever touch them. In the eyes of the unwise... their going looks like a disaster... but they are in peace... and will live with God in Love."

3.5—Hospice's Meeting of the Fears of Pain, Indignity, and Dying Alone

Those with faith (or a prior NDE experience) are not afraid of passing over to the other side in death but they are afraid of the process of dying, of the body's being out of their control with high pain levels, being humiliated, and being cut off from loved ones in the care of strangers and causing great medical expenses.

When Hospice care is involved, death at home is more likely where both the patient and family can have more control over the process. Elizabeth Kubler-Ross emphasized the ideals of "death with dignity" and pain management shared by Hospice with the family involved in the patient's care as they all prepare for death viewed as a normal transition like the other transitions that happen in the family context of birth, graduation, marriage. The economic costs of death are reduced by hospice care.

With Hospice in the home, there is one family caregiver, usually the spouse, who provides the primary care for the dying person supported by specially trained nurses. Home-based care produced a greater sense of burden, (esp. on the main caregiver) but home-based care provided better feelings of control for both the patient and the family.

After the death of the terminally ill patient, Hospice also provides support for the grief and stress of the caregivers in the family, including spiritual support.

3.6—Healing the Grief Losses of Love and Power

The first stage of grief in losing a loved one is either denial or Numbness as defenses to help the mourner survive emotionally. What follows is a loss of emotional control which may include weeping, expressions of anger and anxiety. There is a deep yearning (love) that the lost person could return.

Facing loss takes our breath away. Our bodies can't take it in and we can't accept the reality of the loss. We are stunned, shocked, unable to take in the magnitude of the loss.

The grieving person will soon desire to withdraw and disengage from others and activities they regularly enjoyed. Feelings of pining and intense yearning give way to periods of apathy, an absence of emotion, and despair showing the mourner's powerlessness in the loss of their loved one.

In the recovery stage, feelings of sadness and despair decrease while positive memories of the deceased begin to increase as the grieving person begins to return to a new state of "normal" with energy levels increasing (power), and an interest to return to enjoyable activities (love investment possible). Grief never ends completely but will be manageable. Receiving bereavement counseling and joining bereavement support groups can help the grieving individual.

The major task of grief is accepting the reality of the loss which is coming full face with the reality that the person is dead and will not return. Without accomplishing this, the grieving person will not be able to continue through the mourning process. Next there is a working through the pain because grief is painful, physically and emotionally. It is important to acknowledge the pain and not suppress it.

The third task is adjusting to the new environment in which the deceased is missing. This may require adjusting to the roles that the deceased once carried out. If it is a spouse that has died, it requires the bereaved to accept their new identity as a "widow" and what this means socially and personally over time.

Finally, good grief requires an emotional relocation of the deceased in order to move on. While the bereaved will never be compelled to totally give up on the relationship, the goal is to find an appropriate place in their emotional lives for the deceased. This requires a letting go of attachments so new relationships can begin to form.

Other researchers suggest that the dying process includes other "themes" such as terror, uncertainty, rescue fantasizes, incredulity, fear of pain for the person dying.

3.7—Coping with the fear Death for Seniors Through Religion

Seniors think and talk more about death than anyone else which leads to less fear and anxiety than those at midlife just facing their mortality as real.

Adults who are religious are less afraid of death because they tend to view death as a positive transition from one life to another more like a graduation than the total destruction of the person. Religion provides adults with death stories that help them cope with their own deaths. Adults who have accomplished goals or believe they have become the person they set out to be have less fear of death. Belief that life has purpose or meaning reduces the fear of death which supports Erikson's theory of ego integrity versus despair.

Death rituals help family members and friends manage grief by giving a specific set of roles to play with both expected and prohibited behaviors. The role content differs markedly from culture to culture but in all cases these rituals bring family members together like no other occasion, inspire shared reminiscences and renew family relationships. They can strengthen family ties, and clarify new roles.

Funerals establish shared milestones for families. Ceremony and ritual can help survivors understand the meaning of death itself.

Widows who have cared for spouses will have normal grief but are less likely to show depression after death. Death that has intrinsic meaning reduces grief. Sudden and violent deaths evoke more intense grief responses. Becoming a widow has immediate and long term effects on the immune system. Immune system responses were suppressed initially after death and do not return to normal up ntil a year later. The incidence of depression among widows and widowers rises substantially. but the length of depression may be highly variable depending upon mental health history, social support, quality of relationship with spouse, and economic changes.

Depression-like symptoms following the death of a loved one that last longer than two months are seen as a clinical issue. Grief lasting longer than 6 months can lead to long-term depression and/ or physical ailments such as cancer and heart disease.

The death of a spouse is more negative for men than for women and there is a greater risk of death from natural causes or suicide immediately after the death of spouse. Widowers withdraw from social activities and find it difficult to return to earlier levels of emotional functioning with alcohol abuse playing a role in higher levels of depression.

The Talk-it-out" approach to managing grief can be helpful in preventing grief-related depression including the development of a coherent personal narrative of the events surrounding the spouse's death. Participating in support groups helps as well as taking the appropriate amount of time off from work to grieve.

3.8—Becker's "Immortality Project" as Denial of Death and False Heroism

The non-theist, Ernest Becker, has written about secular man's "Denial of Death" through symbolic defense systems which seek "immortality projects". Becker sees human civilization as a "symbolic defense mechanism" against the truth of our mortality, Humanity has both physical selves and symbolic selves and it is through our symbolic selves we can transcend our mortality through the (false) "heroism" of our "immortality project". People believe that they can become part of something eternal when they become heroic to be part of something eternal, part of something that will never die which in turn, gives people the feeling that their lives have significance in the grand scheme of things. (Becker). When our hero system fails us, we live in the shadow of death and become mentally ill with depression or anxiety and when our immortality projects contradict each other, quasi-religious wars develop.

Becker claims that the traditional "hero-systems" of religion, are no longer convincing in the age of reason but that science will never be able to solve the problem of our mortality. Instead we need new convincing "illusions" that enable us to feel heroic and immortal but Becker has no solution except to say that we must face that there is mortality with no real evidence for immortality. Becker's book was written so well he received the Pulitzer Price two years after his death for expressing so well the angst of modern man in the face of the ultimacy of death. Perhaps winning the Pulitzer price is a type of "immortality project" but his book will not answer Zorba's urgent questions: why do we die and where do we go.

3.9—Tillich's Existential Search for an Ultimacy Beyond Death

The philosophy of Existentialism has been sought by both theists and non-theists in their attempt to find meaning and purpose in the face of total annihilation. Existentialism encourages a realistic awareness of the death, especially one's own death, wherein something ultimate and absolute is encountered in its negative form which is the destruction of the body in physical death. To offset the tragic impact of death, man must find something that is equally ultimate and absolute. In all the major religions, this ultimacy is a God whose love and power is greater than physical death. One existential answer is attempted by Paul Tillich.

Paul Tillich identifies three kinds of death threats in life: physical suffering and death, the moral suffering from guilt and condemnation, and the spiritual suffering of meaninglessness. Tillich sees "ultimate concern" as the power of life to respond to every form of death because life is connection to "the Ground of Being" as its source and destiny. Thus Tillich calls the battle between the life and death forces as "being vs nonbeing". Christ is an answer to these three challenges to the fullness of life, three forms of "nonbeing".

Tillich believed that the gap between the ultimacy of God and man's anxious finitude is bridged by the **"New Being" of Jesus the Christ** who has conquered physical death, moral condemnation, and the loss of meaning in life. Jesus' resurrection was a tangible victory over physical death and his sacrificial death as both man and God was a release/forgiveness from moral condemnation. This New Being of Christ establishes an all surpassing meaning in the midst of tragedy and injustice because all losses are reversed by His resurrection from the dead to be given to all of us. Therefore the Be-attitudes can dare to say: "Blessed (happy) are they that mourn", "blessed (happy) are they who are persecuted in the sake of justice". These are spiritual paradoxes that defy logic.

3.8—The Buddhist Cosmology Bridging Science and Religion

The existential issues of death, meaninglessness in the face of death, and evil in the world were the conditions that gave rise to Buddhism. The dark side of human existence (the insatiable greed, the blatant dishonesty, the disastrous corruption, the cold-blooded violence). How can one be happy in our limited youth, health, and life when all these inevitably lead to the old age, sickness and death of our "human condition" ("Dukha") The systematic problem-solving of Buddhism is based on logic more than faith. Suffering is the problem and the answer is expressed as "Four Noble Truths".

The first Noble Truth is that life involves suffering because we are part of the human condition. The 2nd truth tells us that the cause of suffering is within ourselves: "our imbalanced cravings" for things that are not ultimate which lead to passions, hatred, violence. The 3rd noble truth is to decrease and balance our desires in order to decrease our suffering. The 4th Noble Truth answers the big question of "how we decrease our attachments" by turning us to the "Eightfold Path" to achieve spiritual fitness.

We seek happiness in things that are impermanent and become unhappy with the loss of something desired. The solution is to find something permanent. The "morality, concentration and wisdom" of the Eightfold Path empty us of self-centeredness and fills us with a compassion that allows the individual to serve with a purity free of attachments or self-motives. The Eightfold Path" purifies" all aspects of the individual through practicing an holistic "rightness" in every aspect of our lives: right thinking, right attitudes, right action habits, right livelihood.

Right effort is needed to remove us from bad habits combined with right "mindfulness" to keep our thinking "right" leading to the eighth step of right meditation to "transcend our restless nature through a quieting of the mind."

Following this path of right wholeness will eventually lead to an enlightenment of an inner reality that is transcendent and a source of permanence. In the interim, doing more good than harm will decrease bad karma and increase good karma to decrease our suffering if we must be reincarnated to try again for the ultimate release into Nirvana (the eternal bliss).

Buddhist ethics focus on the three root evils of greed, hatred and delusion which need to be reversed by their opposites of generosity/renunciation, compassion/kindness and insight/truth. (Fisher, p138). According to Buddhism, Nirvana is more transcendent than our limited experiences of gods or demons. Although Buddha shows the way to Nirvana, he is not a god but a guide and model for spiritual fitness and transformation.

Every religious worldview, has a cosmic dimension beyond science when it talks of life after death. Buddhism is more user friendly to science than Christianity because the Buddha never claimed to be a god or reveal a god. The ideas of gaining and losing karma make economic sense to the Western mind wherein you gain money for the good and lose money for bad investments. Lacking any acceptable afterlife view, secularity prefers this impersonal system of life/death. This brings us to a consideration of the metaphysical and ethical perspectives of Christianity with its emphasis on the power of love over the love of power.

CHAPTER FOUR

RELIGIOUS VISIONS OF DIVINE POWER AND LOVE

4.1—Power and Love in the Cosmic Creation via Quantum Physics

Quantum Physics allows a transcendence over the very different narratives between Genesis and Darwin. Darwin's non-theism forced an improbable conclusion that the unfolding of species was without an overall intelligence as if impersonal chance could design such an intelligent order. As the scientist and philosopher Aristotle noted: when dumb things (lacking brains) observe an intelligent order, the order is designed and maintained by an intelligence - even if unseen. The empirical bias and the limited paradigm of science has knocked the invisible Maker of the Universe out of the equation. The Cosmic physicist, Brian Swimme, following the new vision of Quantum Physics has brought God back into the cosmic order, but focuses on what is seen and calls this intelligent source and sustainer: the "Universe celebrating" from the Big Bang forward into the unfolding of life.

The universe unfolded in a sequence over 14 billion years from the release of hydrogen and helium to the development of one-celled life according to Brian Swimme. (Universe Story, p264). What followed the big bang was not just random explosions of matter but a "celebration omnipresent in the grandeur of the entire cosmic process." (Ibid.) The great variety of plants and animals that unfolded on our earth were so rich as to have an "exuberance and joy in being".

With mammal life, an intimate connection developed with babies born within the mother and bonded to her until self-sufficient. Finally, intelligent and self-conscious life was developed and all the above manifestations were reflections of an unseen, intelligent, intimate guidance which defies the probabilities of chance. The guidance behind the universe was patiently purposeful. The universe is a "single, multiform, sequential, celebratory event" with a "certain exuberance and joy in being"...pressing toward expanded modes of being with ever more intimate presence of things to each other." (Ibid.)

The proper response to this awesome unfolding is to CELEBRATE God's love and power with exuberance and joy for the grandeur and beauty of the purposeful and patient intelligence behind the universe coming out of nothingness... "in the Beginning..." was an explosion of light that would become a source of life.

The key moments of our cosmic unfolding together were first the implosive of the first stars to release the elements needed to support life systems 14 billion years ago. Another milestone was when cells of plants became able to turn the energy of the sun into a life-supporting substance through photosynthesis. The flower revolution afforded animals quick protein consumed quickly to free up time leading to new transformations until man is able to enter into the larger community of life. "Our individual self finds its most complete realization within our family self and eventually our universe self." (Ibid.)

Man was "at home" in the natural world seeing the power and splendor of the universe as part of a sacred cosmos and early man sought to find the pre-existing order in nature to align himself with the rhythms, purposes and seasons of scarcity or abundance, drought or rainfall, heat and cold. But men were also victims to the powers in nature of earthquakes, cyclones, volcanoes, hurricanes, natural disasters and tried to placate these forces with sacrifices. Bad things could happen to good people in this universe and for some this negated their concept of a good, all loving God. These incongruities continue to puzzle the modern world.

Nevertheless, a coherent purpose was sustained over the course of 14 billion years to develop a planet that would support life, amass the right chemicals for the leap into primitive micro-life that would develop into sentient life of mammals and primates and finally the intelligence of man, beyond random chance. Swimme integrates the facts of science with a spiritual vision consistent with our ancient wisdom tradition.

4.2— God's Power of Love and Powers Against Love

One major challenge causing people to flee from a "Secure Connection" with the Maker of the Universe is that tragic "acts of God" (forest fires, floods, earthquakes, tornadoes, hurricanes) happen to good people who do not seem to have "bad karma". Ancient people thought that sacrifices of various kinds (substitutes for human) were needed to appease angry nature gods. The Book of Job was a Jewish argument refuting the idea that all suffering is caused by sin (or bad karma) and that there will be times when bad things happen to good people. Psalm 22 of David begins "My God, my God, why have you forsaken me" a good man while evil men prosper? This was the same Psalm that Jesus cited as he was dying on the Cross. For both David and Jesus, the Psalm ends with faith in God's reputation to turn around bad things for a greater good.

A more personal "power against love" experience is when believers come to see God as a perfectionistic judge whom we can never satisfy so that we are always in danger of His wrath and condemnation which can even lead to suffering after life. Martin Luther was a perfectionist himself with an angry, demanding human father who projected his father's wrath onto God to cut him off from God's love. Erik Erikson looked at Luther's spiritual peaks and pits through his developmental perspective. Luther could find no peace from his obsessive perfectionism (confessing for hours) until he discovered Paul's revelation (Romans) that we are saved by faith and not by our fulfilling the law so that for those who believe there is "therefore no condemnation" (Romans 12). Luther had distorted his view of God with own lack of forgiveness for his father taken as a false ultimate (a false god) until the impact of God's love broke and transcended the anger both to and from his father.

Luther imagined that God's caused His Son to die on the cross because of a perfectionistic power demand. As Luther was able see that the Father's love transcended all anger and condemnation, he could understand the Father's identification with a suffering son and his son suffering to bring humanity over the divide of sin that had separated us from secure attachment. Secure attachment to God lets us find forgiveness quickly when we fall short of the mark and allows us to trust him even when we go through the valley of the shadow (the pits).

Paul saw the legalism of the law as a source of disconnection from God as we focus on making ourselves righteous (God-like) with self sufficient power instead of receiving the completed gift of Jesus taking all the karmic debt upon himself and paying in advance so that guilt would not separate us from God's love. If God is moral perfection, the sinfulness keeps man far from intimacy (love) with God until he is either punished enough or perfected enough. Man's moral weakness will keep him from either becoming punished enough or perfect enough. How could the enormous chasm between perfection and imperfection be closed?

4.3—Legalistic Power Balanced by the Grace of Agape Love

The cosmology of Christian grace is rooted in the Jewish system of legalism.

Jesus was born an Jew, claims to have fulfilled the Jewish law at a higher spiritual level, and never rejected His Jewishness even after His Resurrection. (And after all this time I thought that He was a Catholic!) Paul brings both continuity and change from the Jewish tradition and provides the original theology of the New Testament.

The symbolic world of Judaism focused on Temple, Torah, Territory and Truth. We are Israel, the true people of the true God but our God. The evidence of our truth is that we exercise justice within and fight evil outside against the pagan nations surrounding us. Israel's true covenant with God is confirmed both in their suffering at the hands of pagan nations and in God's victories over these nations. Israel was a true light against the darkness of the pagan idolatry. According to Paul, Israel's prideful legalism had fallen short of true righteousness to break their side of the covenant. Alas, the truly chosen had fallen into external appearances. Legalism became a new form of idol worship (a false god of appearances). God does not want fasting from food but fasting from abusing your workers on the Sabbath. God wants true worship in the spirit of the law that breaks the heart of sin, not a coverup of false righteousness mixed with hypocrisy.

The old Covenant had been ratified by God's deliverance of His people out of Egyptian bondage into the promised land. Hallelujah! A new covenant was now needed to deliver both Jews and Gentiles out of legalistic bondage into the freedom of faith. This time the deliverance is through the sacrificial death of the Messiah Jesus. According to Paul, the vindication of Israel's covenant promise is the Resurrection of Christ. As Messiah, Jesus now represents Israel as a whole. Death is the penalty of sin but Israel's defeat of death through their Messiah's Resurrection finally fulfills God's covenant promise that Israel would be restored. Abraham's faith was considered by God as righteousness and now this same righteousness by faith was being given both to Jews and Gentiles. Righteousness was no longer limited by territory or tribe, but the Universal God was given to the human universe for all who believed and lived with authentic truth.

All of humanity, gentiles and Jews, are descendants of Abraham by faith in the Oneness of God grafted into the original Tribe of the Torah.

Paul as a Jewish Christian held on to all the central Jewish doctrines but redefined them in the light of Jesus as the Messiah (the Christ). After the fall of Adam, God's covenant with Abraham was both a paradoxical failure, and a paradoxical success as the Covenant was fulfilled both in failure and in success in the death and resurrection of Jesus which is the source of cosmic renewal. "Oh happy fault that merited us (all) such a precious Redeemer"(Easter Vigil Catholic liturgy). If things hadn't become that bad, we would not ever have had it this good with God incarnate in Christ in the fullness of our humanity. The Power of God's moral perfection had to be sacrificed because man could not rise up either in sufficient sacrifice or sufficient goodness to have union with the Perfect love of God. The only answer was for an all powerful God to become a powerless little human baby in an imperfect world where power-hungry men would seek to kill him. Indeed, Jesus as the God-man would have to bear in his mortal humanity all of God's terrible wrath against the nature of anti-God sin. The enormity of this sacrifice is manifested by the bloodless sacrifice of the mass celebrated every day over all of the Christian and mission-field world over the course of 2,000 years. Imagine bearing all this on one day in a human vessel holding all of God and all of man!

The Exodus led by Moses, Mosaic Law, and the first five books of Moses as the sacred scripture of the Torah were the centerpieces of Jewish religion with the Patriarchs (Abraham, Isaac and Jacob) on one side and the major prophets (such as Isaiah) on the other side. Jesus was raised and grounded in faith as a Jew in all the above as well as the major ritual of Passover. It was the Passover which Jesus celebrated as a new form of deliverance from bondage the night before he died which then became the repeated communion ritual of Christianity (esp. the Catholic communion which is the core of every Mass celebration.)

Following Paul, Christianity continued to be Jewish from its origins and foundation but with a radical reform from legalism to being spirit-led. As Paul said emphatically in Romans 12 that it is by "faith" that we are saved by grace (the unmerited favor of God's love) and not by works. Paul was a Pharisee at the most righteous top of the Jewish hierarchy before a dramatic conversion where he did a full circle from persecuting Christians to dedicating his life to promoting Christianity as an extension of Jewish righteousness into the gentile world at large. He himself was to be an example for the Jewish world at large to have a first hand experience of the Risen Christ.

For the larger mainstream of Judaism, the "suffering servant Messiah of Isaiah "is not enough to validate God's eternal covenant with Israel. The destruction of the six million jews in the Nazi holocaust requires the full messiah known not as the "Son of God" (blasphemy for Jews) but as "the Son of Man" Kings of kings.

4.4—The Power of Messiah Jesus as "the Son of Man"

Throughout the Gospels, Jesus asks the question: "And who do you say that I am?" Jesus did not ask this question to get confirmation or clarity from the outside because the Jews of this oppressed Roman colony often wanted him to be a military revolutionary or provider for all their needs of poverty, sickness, suffering.

Throughout the Gospels, Jesus answers his own question of identity by saying that "I am the Son of Man" EIGHTY TIMES!! The messiah as "the Son of Man" was spoken by Daniel as one who will have "divine dominion, glory and divine kingship" which can never be taken away (Daniel 7:13, M. Kelly, p. 33).

*In his book **Rediscovering Jesus**, Matthew Kelly summarizes the unusual powers of "the Son of Man" which Jesus demonstrated. Jesus showed power of nature in calming the storm and the seas by his command. Jesus showed the power to forgive sins and miracles of healing to valid this power. "Which is easier to say: "Your sins are forgiven you" or "Rise up and walk". "So that you may know that the Son of Man has authority on earth to forgive sins", Jesus healed (and forgave) the paralytic who picked up his stretcher and walked home as the crowds were "STRUCK WITH AWE". (Matt 9:1-7) Kelly asks the question to the reader: "when was the last time you were awestruck by Jesus?" (M. Kelly, p. 35)*

"The Son of Man" is lord even of the Sabbath (Mark 2:27) because the power of Resurrection is above the works of righteousness and Jesus would then raise Lazarus from the dead and say "I am the resurrection and the life, whoever believe in me, even if he dies, will live..."(Jn11:44) The revelation is in the first two words: "I am" the great "I am".

The suffering servant was not enough. The "Son of Man" was to be a king but the kingdom was not of this earth. The Jews needed the kingdom to be of this earth to defeat Roman oppression as well as the moral oppression from the Pharisees. Jesus claims to be God through the set of God-like powers.

The righteousness by faith of Abraham was in the revelation in that God is One, spirit and invisible. Suddenly there is this "incarnation of God" alien to the Jewish tradition. Now the Son of Man revelation is too much and still too otherworldly for the realpolitik needs of the day.

4.5—The Power "Tactics" of Jesus to Empower the Poor and Powerless

Non-believers are skeptical hearing about Jesus from those within the camp on the other side of the cultural and political divide. Jay Haley is a non-believer who sees Christ's "tactics" as revolutionary for empowering the powerless and poor considered of no political consequences by ruling regimes up to the time of Christ when oppressed Christians formed a spiritual army to defeat the great Roman empire without any tangible weapons. Haley reveals the intangible spiritual, psychological and social "weapons" ("tactics") to form a dynasty that would become the "Holy

Roman Empire" and a Roman Catholic church with sectarian reforms that would last 2,000 years.

Haley begins by downsizing the power of Christianity enough to allow the reader to appreciate the awesomeness of the past dinosaur age and to indicate his own detached, secular position interested on in the wise "tactics" of political power.

"Now that Christianity has declined as a force in the world of ideas, we are free to appreciate the skills of Jesus Christ." (Haley, p. 29). Most Christians and social scientists have somehow failed to notice the "incredible" organizing ability of Christ, noting that "no other person has approached such an accomplishment" to take over the Roman Empire and hold power over the Western world for many hundreds of years. The revolutionary tactics of Jesus taught all later revolutionaries of the past century in finding power "by organizing the poor and the powerless". (Haley, p. 30). Perhaps this understanding may shed some light on the political revolution of the right in 2016 if paradoxical parallels may be seen).

The first challenge Christ had was that he came into public life alone and unknown with powerful organizations set to oppose any political insurrection. Jewish orthodoxy had a system of compulsory laws that controlled everyone from birth to death and to oppose this status quo of the conservative rich would set off punishment from Roman rule which ruthlessly exterminated revolutionaries. How was Jesus to gain power in this entrenched system of religious and political control? The answer was to begin to bring to light the everyday problems of the everyday people and bring a consensus of agreement that these were real and shared sources of suffering for the oppressed classes.

Poverty of the Roman colony was made worse by excessive and corrupt taxation systems so bad that the people had little to lose with a major change to the systems supporting the status quo. The ruling powers were themselves divided. The Romans were hated by the Jews and vice versa. The priestly hierarchy had its own internal conflicts over power and principle. The hope against such oppression was the Jewish belief in someone coming in the prophetic tradition who would be the Messiah to deliver Israel into justice and freedom from Rome.

Jesus was outside all the hated systems of power. He was not rich, not a member of the religious hierarchy, and not a Roman. (Haley, p. 32)

Only one track to upward mobility in Judaism was available to Jesus: he could become a wandering religious prophet and the establishment was used to criticism by such prophets and expected to tolerate it. Social change required getting people's attention by giving something new from the old uncorking system and yet not so new as to challenge the people's orthodoxy. Jesus did both by criticizing the shallow inconsistency of the law while pressing in for a deeper fulfillment of the law that would bring greater justice and truth. In short, Jesus was calling both for conformity and change at the same time. "I have not come to destroy the law but to fulfill it" (Matt 5:17). By calling for conformity to the Law, Jesus disarms opposition but by making the the law more spiritual (not just murder but anger a sin), he sets himself up as equal in power to the entire religious establishment. He did not teach like the Scribes but as one having authority and the people were "astonished" by his new teachings. (Haley, p. 36) With the religious authority of prophets, a single man could undo the consensus of politicians by bringing forth a divine revelation which the people receive as true and coming form a higher authority.

Having redefined the law from a higher spiritual level, Jesus could then attack the establishment for deviating from the higher truth. The oppressed would have a voice that expresses their anger toward the unjust rich without being punished because of the respect given to prophets.

Should leaders of great power struggles be enshrined in some hall of fame, Haley votes that the first "niche belongs to the Messiah from Galilee" who was an "extraordinary innovator". (Haley, p. 68)

4.6—Mark's Fast Track Account of Christ's Power in Action

Power marches through the Gospel of Mark as we only follow the events marked by the phrase"immediately". Mark's Gospel skips Christ's birth all the way up to his adult life when he comes from Nazareth to the Jordan River to be baptized by his cousin John.

John is baptizing many who repent of their sins in their recognition of the power of John as a prophet but John says that "ONE MIGHTIER THAN I IS COMING. I have baptized you in water, but he will baptize you with the Holy Spirit.

JESUS comes to be baptized by John in the Jordan and IMMEDIATELY he saw the heavens opening up...and there came a voice from the heavens, "YOU ARE MY BELOVED SON. IN YOU AM I WELL PLEASED." Those observers who saw a dove descend from on high and heard the voice believed this voice to be the most powerful Maker of the Universe revealed to Abraham as the One God behind all the many creations in the earth and beyond. This One God calls Jesus "My Son".

As Cosmic physics describes the vast awesomeness of the Universe, we all would love to have some personal knowledge of this impersonal but intelligent power and suddenly there is this revelation 2,000 years and major religions have kept this most unusual event in memory.

No sooner is Jesus baptized when IMMEDIATELY the Spirit drives him forth into the desert where he will be tempted for 40 days by Satan. Our modern world does not want to believe in Satan but science has no explanation for the evil that abounds every day in the papers with drugs, murders, the mass violence of ISIS.

The Bible minces no words but shows that the terrible affairs in planet earth is due to a battle between the forces of goodness and evil, of light and darkness, as fallen angels try to play god and upstage God's plan. The modern world would prefer the science fiction battles of "Star Wars" or "The Hunger Games" but we watch many different forms of good vs evil battles on all our TV channels with the conclusion that some people choose evil while others choose good and therein is an ongoing battle.

Jesus then begins choosing his helpers, not from the top rungs of society, but among lowly, simple fishermen when he says, 'COME FOLLOW ME and I will make you "fishers of men". AND IMMEDIATELY they left their nets and followed Jesus. Later other fishermen were mending nets and IMMEDIATELY Jesus called to them...and they followed him.

Although Jesus has chosen humble and lowly followers, he must confront the highest powers of religious establishment. So IMMEDIATELY on the Sabbath, Jesus went into the synagogue and began to teach them and they were astonished at his teaching and his authority. (spiritual power) Doctors were few in these days, and prophets proved themselves with "signs and wonders" to heal and cast out demons. Jesus did cure many diseases and cast out many devils. (healing power) One demon said "I know who you are - the Holy One of God." Even the demons confirm that Jesus has power both on earth and in the supernatural regions and has a close connector to the Almighty Creator.

THE HEROIC RESILIENCE OF HAPPINESS

Lepers were the untouchables but Jesus had compassion on a leper, touched him and when he spoke IMMEDIATELY the leprosy left him and he was made clean. The popularity of Jesus grew and people with various afflictions sought him out. When one group couldn't get close to Jesus for healing, the cut a hole in the roof and lowered a paralytic into the room where Jesus was staying. Jesus said to the paralytic "I say to thee arise and go to thy house. AND IMMEDIATELY he arose in everyone's sight and they were all amazed saying "Never did we see the like."

But not everyone was pleased by these "signs and wonders" from someone outside the established order. The Pharisee went out and IMMEDIATELY took counsel with the Herodians (followers of Herod) against him how they might do away with him.

If healings aren't surprising enough, Jesus comes to the bedside of a dead 12 year old girl, took her hands and said "Girl, I say to thee, arise". And the girl rose up IMMEDIATELY and began to walk. We know later that Jesus will raise Lazarus from the dead and these are major miracles unmatched by religious leaders but foreshadowing that Jesus himself will be raised from the dead.

More signs and wonders when Jesus was preaching to a large crowd at supper time and realized everyone was hungry. Jesus took five loaves and two fishes and he fed 5,000 men. IMMEDIATELY after this miracle, he made his disciples get into the boast and cross the sea ahead of him while he dismissed the crowd and went to the mountain to pray and he came walking on the Sea and his disciples were troubled thinking this was ghost. Jesus IMMEDIATELY spoke to them saying "Be not afraid" and got in the boat with them and they were utterly beside themselves with astonishment. Jesus wanted to help their faith with many signs and wonders that could only come from God because the minds of his apostles could not grasp what was happening.

While in Jerusalem, a woman whose child had an unclean spirit IMMEDIATELY came in and fell at the feet of Jesus and the child was delivered. Clearly some healing were medical while others were deliverance from possession by evil spirits. An example of a medical healing was when a deaf man's ears were opened and IMMEDIATELY he could hear and the bond of his tongue loosed.

Followers came to see signs and wonders, be healed and delivered and even be fed but Jesus said "let him deny himself and take up his cross to follow me. He who would save his life will lose it, but he who loses his life for the Gospel's sake will save it." Jesus was a suffering servant who showed that eternal life would be for those willing to follow in his footsteps to serve those suffering and battle all the powers of evil "for the sake of the Gospel", to bring God's inner Kingdom.

4.7—John's Gospel on the Inner Power of the Love of Christ

*In contrast to Mark's rapid move of God's Messianic revolution, John shows the inner spiritual revolution through the power of love to establish God's Kingdom within. Love for Mark is an **activity** of healing, deliverance, redemption from different forms of evil while love for John is a sustained transforming interaction with the person of Christ.*

John's Gospel shows the deep intimate love of Jesus of transaction which converts hearts so that they can be moved to action following the one they come to know and love. Consider the 1st letter letter of John establishing the sequence: we come to know love through God who loves us first and then we keep our "secure connection" to a God whom we do not see by loving those whom we do see and see so well that love is a challenge needing grace.

"Let us love one another for love comes from God. Everyone who loves has been born of God and knows God. Whoever does not love, does not know God because God is love." Not only does God love but love is God's essence, the core of who God is. How did God show this love you may ask and John answers:

"God showed his love among us when he sent his one and only Son into the world that we might live through him. This is love. Not that we loved God but that God first loved us (when we were not so lovable) and sent his Son as an atoning sacrifice (to make us more lovable) for our sins"

Just as Mark was the sudden movement of "immediately, the Book of John is an invitation to a "love-in" based on the first hand experience of the apostle John who had the most time of any of the apostles to find the lasting impact of Christ's personal love as a light for all men in darkness. Love first appears as the light of Christ's love in the primordial darkness and the current darkness of sin in every age.

According to John, Jesus was the primordial light which shone in the darkness which could not comprehend it. Jesus was the "True Light who gives light to every man who comes into the world. The Law was given by Moses but "grace and truth came through Jesus Christ."

"For God (the Greatest lover) so loved the world (the greatest love) that He gave His only begotten Son (the greatest love offering) that whosoever believes in Him (the greatest invitation to love) should not perish but have everlasting life (the greatest gift of Love). (Quoted from Anonymous commentary).

For God did not send His Son into the world to **condemn** the world which are the love obstacles of guilt and fear. Instead Jesus came into the world to free us from the law by grace that we might be saved through our free choice of faith. He who believes in Jesus is not condemned (Jn 16-18) but rejection of Christ leaves us in the darkness. "Light has come into the world but men loved darkness more than the light to hide their evil deeds in darkness. He who loves the truth comes to the light to be clearly seen for deeds done in God. God is Spirit and the Light of truth and those who worship Him must worship God both in Spirit and in truth. Jn4:24

If the Son of Man makes you free, you shall be free indeed. The thief comes to steal, kill and to destroy. I have come that you may have life and that you may have it abundantly. (Jn 10:10). These things I have spoken to you that My joy may remain in you and that your joy may be full. (Jn15:11)

John admits the problem that "No one has ever seen God" but he claims that "if we love each other, God lives in us and his love is made complete in us."

If you abide in my Word, you are my disciples indeed. 8:31 If we abide in love by practicing it regularly we develop a "secure attachment" to God because God IS LOVE itself in its fullness. When we struggle with our faith because we cannot feel God's presence, we need to love our neighbor, someone near and dear or maybe the one who needs love and is hard to love. (4:7, 4:16) We love God by carrying out his LOVE commandments and thus do God's will.

"Oh dear Lord, three things I pray. To hear you more clearly (to know your will), to follow you more nearly(to do your will) and to love your more dearly day by day (by actively loving a tough, real, active love of others). (**Godspell** song)

John goes on to say that love is a remedy for fear. "There is no fear in God's unconditional agape love because "Perfect Love" casts out all fear when fear is connected to punishment. The man who fears has not yet been made perfect in (God's) love (4:18) and is not fully persuaded that the perfect sacrifice of Jesus the Messiah has saved us from sin punishment to the utmost. Mosaic law set up punishments for sin leading to men focusing on external appearances of righteousness and hypocrisy as no human can be perfect before the law. Grace was needed to bridge the gap between our imperfections and God's perfect holiness.

Where Mark's Gospel repeats "immediately", John's Gospel repeats Christ's words about the importance of maintaining secure attachment with God through His incarnate Son.

4.8—Augustine's Vision of Grace as the Access to Love

Augustine, like Paul found Christ through a conversion, led by the voice of a child speaking the advice of Paul "to put on the fullness of Christ" at a time when Augustine felt especially lost in the lawlessness of worldliness.

Augustine looked for love in all the wrong places (power, sexuality, success) and in the end discovered that the happiness of love was inseparable from **goodness.** We must become "enchanted with the radiance of goodness, to find it compelling and irresistible" in order to be transformed by goodness. We must begin with the "befriending activity of God through **grace** because our moral life begins in grace, grows in grace and is sustained by grace. We learn to respond to this grace in freedom in order to cooperate with it because grace involves a "partnership" with others (and God,) working with receptivity and cooperation.

We seek to be self-sufficient but we must work in harmony with God's grace so that our souls can be transformed into the character of Christ. (Wadel, p. 6) Augustine concludes that "our hearts are restless" until they find their rest in God's love because we can only find our fulfillment in loving and serving the God who made us in His Image. In short, "the happy life is to love God wholeheartedly and faithfully because God is our supreme and most excellent good as expressed in Augustine's prayer below.

> "O Beauty Ever Ancient, O Beauty Ever New".
> Oh late have I loved you, oh late have I turned,
> turned from seeking you in creatures...
> things you fashioned as a pathway,

yet I lost myself in them...
By your grace you have renewed me,
let me live my life in you!
(The Confessions of St. Augustine).

Power, fame and sexual affairs all left Augustine empty lacking the happiness love he so desired. On the verge of a breakdown, he admitted his powerlessness to achieve the love he desired so desperately. Grace came to him through a child's voice telling him "put on the Lord Jesus Christ" as described in Paul. (Wadell, p9). In that moment, Augustine experienced a sudden, unexpected bliss, not from his own efforts, but as a gift of grace. Augustine was baptized 387 A.D. at the age of 33 when he realized that happiness comes from grace as a un-merited gift of God's love.

All religions are systems of effort according to laws wherein man achieves his own salvation. However, the Christian view is that our salvation is given to us by grace through the perfect sacrifice of Christ. We show our love and gratitude to Christ by our good works of loving charity and service.

4.9—Aquinas' View of Union with God by Living in Christ's Love

Augustine's worldview led to the contrast between the lost human world and the saved world of God's kingdom which dominated the Christian worldview through the middle Ages until the humanism of Aristotle was rediscovered by Aquinas to bridge the two worlds. For Aquinas, sharing intimacy with God continuously until perfect communion is achieved is our ultimate human longing.

Like Augustine, Aquinas considered the possible sources of happiness (pleasure, success, status) and saw that all contribute to quality of life but none of these bring us our **optimal excellence** as human beings. We are only fulfilled by something that surpasses us because our ultimate good must stretch us, carry us beyond previous levels of growth, something that we possess in the deepest possible way. As humans we seek that an **all-surpassing goodness** beyond the imperfections of this world.

Since we are made to seek intimacy with God, how can we do this as humans since God is only goodness? We must become good and do good to be in fellowship with God, and develop an intimate friendship with God. Nothing less than God can fill the God-sized hole in our souls.

Knowing that we want union with God, how can we do this since we know we cannot achieve moral goodness by our own efforts alone? Aquinas agrees with Augustine that God's grace is needed but adds that grace comes as we live a life of charity: a life of love, friendship and communion with fellow humans.

*Aquinas believes that every person begins life with the **gift of God's love** already poured into our hearts. We already have the love we need but we have it imperfectly, see it dimly and can lose it unless we have loving communities and spiritual mentors until we can learn and develop into the character of Christ with Jesus as our primary Mentor. In short, to know true love we need to become disciples of Christ: listening to his word, knowing his deeds, imitating his example and ultimately become one in union with the love of God in Christ. Living a life doing good (good works for those in need) is evidence of the love of God in us.*

4.10—Toward an Holistic Theory of Truth for Power and Love

Holistic theories are currently sought to offset the fragmented research that does not come together with any coherence. Religious systems of thought have favored an integral wholeness such as the four "Noble Truths" of how to heal our suffering and the "Eight Fold Path" of living rightly. The core of suffering for Buddhism can be stated simply as attachment to what is impermanent. Christians say that we are attached to our sin-nature and need to reattach to Christ who removes sin (evil) and leads us to goodness which is source of happiness. Permanence for Christians is stated in Luther's hymn: "On Christ the solid rock I stand (everlasting permanence) All other ground is sinking sand." (impermanence). Death is the major challenge to permanence. Christ as the God-man experienced human death and was able to conquer death with a resurrection witnessed by his inner circle of apostles many others over the course of forty days.

The power of conversion is another dimension of spiritual power. Paul never knew Christ in the flesh but had a vision of Christ in the spirit that left him helpless for three days during which time he changed

180 degrees from Pharisee elite actively defending the orthodoxy of Judaism into conversion to a religion he had considered blasphemy that he would spread to the gentile world. Such major changes require some scientific explanation because of the cognitive dissonance created by such a paradoxical reversal. Christianity would have a hall of fame full of such radical conversions from Augustine to C.S. Lewis over 2,000 year period.

Our full statement on the holistic views of both power and love await our concluding chapter when our journey is fully completed and explored.

What is evident at this stage is that the exploration of the topics of love and power in relation to heroism and happiness is blatantly incomplete without the one historical figure who is most exceptional in both his perfect love and outstanding supernatural power. The bigger question to be answered is why the socio-political nature of the academic world has turned negative toward Christianity and our own inner forces which resist and resent the blend of power and lover in the historical Christ Jesus. Is it true that we all have some vulnerability to a certain darkness that fights against the inconvenient truths of light manifested In Jesus?

CHAPTER FIVE

HAPPINESS LOVE AND HEROIC POWER FOR ADLER, FREUD & JUNG

5.1—Adler's Spiritual Fitness for Empowerment to Heal Inferiority

Since we are encouraging the reader (and writer) to illustrate the general landscape of the lifespan with their own particular stories, the case studies of the three founders of psychology provide relevant material on power and love. We begin with the power conflict of sibling rivalry leading to inferiority and superiority complexes. Alfred Adler, one of the three founding fathers of modern psychology, was himself stuck in the purgatory of inferiority due his place in sibling competition in his own "family constellation".

Adler's first born brother, Sigmund, was older, stronger, smarter, and healthier in every way over his younger, sickly brother, Alfred. By his own theory, Sigmund Adler was destined toward a "superiority complex" that would motivate him to be a "winner" in most of the contests of life whereas Alfred's inferiority complex would doom him to be a "loser" in sports, academics, business and romance. Rather than giving up because he lost the victories of happiness, Alfred embraced the courage of heroism to fight against the odds inspired by a doctor who helped him regain his health. Adler went on himself to become a doctor and a healer of those afflicted by inferiority complexes. Later Alfred would learn from another superior Sigmund named Freud but go on to make a more equalitarian form of healing alliance between patient and therapist than Freud would allow. Unresolved issues of sibling rivalry can be exported to other relationships both in marriage and career to become battles of proving oneself a "winner" rather than a "loser".

Adler made a distinction between two types of inferiority complex. In the beginning it is in the young child's experience of weakness, helplessness and dependency. Weakness is seen as an evil and thus the child likes to identify with various superheroes who are all powerful ranging from superman to super sports heroes. The original feelings of smallness can be intensified by failed competitions with older and/or more competent siblings, Alfred's illness and younger age made him feel less than in his comparison with a healthy, older brother, Sigmund A.

Adler found that a second level of inferiority when a fictional goal is established in the unconscious as a way to compensate for inferiority which is unattainable and a vicious cycle is set up. Adler faced the facts that he really was inferior in his academic performance. He was inspired by the kind manner of healing achieved by a medical doctor and gained a vision of realistic hope sustained by his virtue of determination and ability to do hard work (disciplined work ethic).

Adler discovered that there is a counterpart of the inferiority complex, which is a "superiority complex" which is equally imbalanced. When Adler became a professional he encountered another "Sigmund" known as Dr. Freud whose "my way or the highway" dogmatism showed a superiority complex that felt short of truth. Freud's system of therapy was as a superior doctor to an inferior patient, but Adler stressed the collaborative, equalitarian roles of doctor and patient as a team needing each other.

In addition to sibling rivalry, children reared in households who were constantly criticized for not living up to parents' expectations also develop an inferiority complex. Adler's therapy begins with nonjudgmental acceptance of the client to help him regain self worth in the context of his own goals and values.

Adler sees inferiority feelings as a motivator to strive for useful activity and progress. The first battle is to break out of the vicious cycle wherein inferior feelings lower self confidence and self esteem to become a self-fulfilling prophesy for the negative. The patient needs to be "encouraged" to have courage to face potential failure by working hard to achieve realistic goals that are not the self-defeating perfectionism of the "all or nothing" irrational thinking. Focusing on the peak areas of one's strengths can compensate to bring up the pits of weaknesses.

Adler's vision of therapy is holistic (like religion and philosophy) rather than the tendency of science to be reductive and compartmentalized. Adler saw the role of confronting negative thinking with positive reframes closer to the truth (cognitive therapy) and translating the positive thoughts into positive actions (behavior therapy) and translating both into healing relationships with affirmations rather than criticisms and judgments, Both Buddhism and Adler present comparable holistic systems of change symbolized by the acronym:

WATCH describes the major power components of Truth:

> **Words, Actions, Talk** (interactions), **Character** (virtues) and **Habits of Heroism** (discipline) which then determine the level of happiness. Integrity is the courage to find truth in the midst of trouble and is a key component of heroism.

An holistic understanding of truth includes the whole person: mind, body, heart and soul. A delay in the normal achievement of lifespan goals can bring negative feelings of loss, frustration and discouragement requiring the encouragement of courageous action against fears of failure. A major obstacle in normal resilience is the distorted faulty thinking of false ultimates along the lines of all or nothing."If I have the right job, I'll be happy. If I don't I will never be happy and right now it looks like I'll never find a job." "If I find my soul mate, I'll live happily ever after. If I don't, nothing else can ever make me happy in life."

Adler's approach can also be integrated into the "Higher Power" of the 12 step program of recovery because of its openness to spirituality. While teaching comparative therapies to undergraduate psychology majors in an inner city university, the following "rap" emerged integrating Adler's battle with the superiority complex and the need for help from a "Higher Power".

A Righteous Rap to 'Fred Adler's Keeping the Main Thing Main: "My homie Fred so old he's dead but what he said is really true now. One day *you're up, next day you're down, one day a smile but the next day's a frown.*

Every loss is a pain, and you can't see no gain unless you keep the main thing MAIN: Your Higher Power will keep you sane.

You hit a home run and you feel like number one. Comes those strike threes and you're down on your knees. Your Higher Power is with you in your lowest hour. Accept your downs and surrender your crowns to Higher Power.

The pain of feeling small began with our first Fall. You are not alone because it happened to us all. When we feel so bad we can get real mad that our mouths talk trash making friendships crash. Higher power will get you sane just keep the main thing MAIN. In the midst of despair, Higher Power will be there. Not alone but a pair surrounded by loving care. With Love face to face, you're freed from your disgrace to pick yourself up to run the good race by Higher Power's Amazing Grace." (original by the author)

5.2—Freud's Courage to Seek Empowerment Beyond Societal Repression

Just as Adler took his own encounter, suffering and conquest of the inferiority complex coming from his family constellation, the center piece of Freud's theory is the shocking repressed secret of the Oedipal complex in the family triad. In Victorian Austria, the father was often the distant bread earner and disciplinarian while the mother was a stay at home nurturer. Such was the case for Freud and to make matters worse, his mother was unusually young and attractive. As a preschool child, Freud had his mom to himself throughout the day only to have his time taken away by his father upon his return from work with the job of enforcing any punishment for bad behavior. In his new level of development, the young Freud could fantasize eliminating his rival so that he could have sole and uninterrupted possession. This "sole possession" was like a fantasy marriage and the defeat of his rival was like a murder mini-plot. If acted out, both parts of this fantasy would destroy the most essential unit of the family and thus the entire matter was unconsciously put away through repression bringing a pit of guilt which could not be relieved until the secret was revealed. As the patient came to see the truth as Freud interpreted projections onto the therapist, the shocking truth could be shared in a non-judgmental atmosphere of trust. Truth for Freud was going beyond the Victorian repression of basic biological needs: breast feeding, potty training, dealing with sexual longings and jealousy.

Freud's main contribution was in the area of hidden and distorted sexuality which gave power to the unconscious to cause behavior contrary to the core values of the actor. Freud took the taboo subject of sexuality and opened the door for greater honesty, research and truth in this area. Simplistic misinterpretations of Freud bringing sex into the light have been used to justify an overindulgence and lack of discipline in this area to which Fromm (and other Neo-Freudians) have warned for a more middle path of balanced restraint between repression and reckless indulgence.

Although Freud focused on the love side of our topic, he himself was a figure of considerable power and dominance in the orthodoxy of his approach that he demanded of his followers. Basically, it was "my way or the highway" for his followers. Both Adler and Jung had to find their own highways of truth into new vistas building on Freud's unique insights and the courage to challenge the norms of the time.

The impact of Freud has moved Western culture out of a repressive Puritanism into greater honesty but also into periods of promiscuity and the weakening of marriage bonds. Neo-Freudians like Eric Fromm have corrected the Freudian ideal of freedom from all repression as a peak state to a state of sexual addiction and confusion. Fromm saw sexual love in the context of marriage as an "art" requiring a deep commitment to one person and a discipline to reveal the mystery of intimacy with that beloved other.

Fromm, Adler and Carl Jung were three followers of Freud who also corrected Freud's identification of religion as a pit (bondage, illusion) into a peak guiding the higher and more mature self which could not happen with living at the biological level wherein sex is just entertainment to do whenever it feels good. Jung saw the role of heroism to help man be transformed from a fragmented lower self (like a caterpillar) to a more integrated whole and higher self (like a butterfly).

Today one of the most researched contribution of Freud is in marriage counseling attachment theory which shows the positives of secure attachment and the challenged relationships of insecure attachments.

5.3—Attachment Theory's View of Power and Love Battles in Marriage

Attachment theory shows how the various breakdowns in attachment lead to dysfunctional dyads in marriage as expressed in the book, How We Love *by M & K Yerkovich with these five problem types:* **Avoider, Pleaser, Vacillator, Controller, and Victim**, *and the most healthy type is the "**Secure Connector**". All of the problem attachments have problems with boundaries (power) or connection (love).*

The Avoider says "No" to connection while the Controller says "No' to boundaries. The Avoider fears connection because he/she has a hard time setting and enforcing boundaries and fears being overtaken or controlled by the other. When an Avoider or Pleaser is dominated by a Controller of some variety, either of these may fall into the role of the "Victim". A different kind of irrational power is manifested by the emotionality of the Vacillator who fears being alone or abandoned and demands that their partner stay connected to the peaks and pits of their emotional roller coaster style and is most frustrated by the Avoider.

The **"Avoider"** says: "I like people, but I'm not very comfortable when they get emotional. I like to keep it simple... it's so much easier when people just take care of themselves. The Avoider often comes from affection-less homes which emphasized independence and self-reliance so that Avoiders grew up learning to just take care of themselves. The problem is that they minimize their feelings and needs in order to deal with the anxiety of having too little nurturing. The avoider needs to learn to set boundaries, express needs and find a method of self-nurturing.

"Vacillators" feel like no one understands their needs. They experience high levels of emotional stress and internal conflict so they want to pick a fight and not know why. Conflict is the last thing Avoiders want but they feel like they are walking on eggshells around Vacillators.

Vacillators grew up with unpredictable parents so that their needs weren't top priority. Without consistent parental affection, they developed feelings of abandonment. As adults, Vacillators are on a quest to find the consistent love they never received as children. They idealize new relationships, but then get tired of them once life and their mate is less than perfect. (Yerkovich's **How We Love**)

"**Pleasers**" might be a variation on the theme of Avoiders who deal with disagreement by giving in and quickly moving on. Like Avoiders, Pleasers have difficulty with confrontation or conflict which makes them less than truthful.

"Pleasers usually grow up in a home with an overly protective or angry critical parent. Pleaser children do everything they can to "be good" to appease their troublesome parent. As adults, Pleasers tend to monitor moods to keep everyone happy but they can become resentful and leave one-sided relationships.

"**Controllers**" make sure they are in charge so they won't be taken advantage of. "Controllers need control to keep vulnerable, negative feelings that they experienced in childhood from surfacing in their adult lives. Having control means having protection from the feelings of fear, humiliation and helplessness. Anger is the one emotion that is not vulnerable, so intimidation and anger are often used to keep control. Control may be highly rigid or more sporadic and unpredictable, but Controllers rarely realize the real reason they need to be in charge except to stay in their comfort zone.

The counterpart dysfunctional dyad might be the "**Victim**" type who keeps their needs quiet because it is safer to just go with the flow and avoid blow-ups. Victims come from chaotic homes and try to be as invisible as possible to lessen the pain from their angry, violent, chaotic parents.

As children, some Victims build whole imaginary worlds in their heads where they can escape the pain of abuse. Victims lack self-worth, and are often anxious and depressed. Victims may replicate their childhood home environment by marrying a Controller and using the coping methods of compliance and retreat to get by.

5.4—Jungian Hero Types Battle Archetypal Losses of Love and Power

Carl Jung found a source of power and fulfillment beyond Freud's personal unconscious into the archetypes of man's collective unconscious. The bottom line for Jung was the "reconciliation of opposites' at our deepest level of symbolic integration of conflict. Christian examples are that life and death are reconciled through Christ's resurrection, human and divine are reconciled by the God/ man Christ, male and female are reconciled through the co-creation of family. For Jung, man's deepest longing (love) is for integrated wholeness through the power to overcome fragmentations and distortions of wholeness.

One fragmentation of our wholeness is a superficial identification with our role in society, which Jung calls our "personna", rather than our "Christ Self" that integrates love of self with the love of the other (self/ other) going beyond me/you to a "we". Christ was a man for others as were his sincere followers that make up a pantheon of saints (holiness heroes). Jung was as positive toward religion as Freud was negative.

Another fragmentation of our wholeness is the negative power of the "shadow" where we hide negative things that we don't want to face. Although we may be embarrassed to face our shadow, this dumpster can also be a treasure chest where our unconscious has discarded something feared but of significant value such as important self insight for growth.

Jung studied a spectrum of symbolic systems from religious systems to folk tales and dreams to find heroes who must leave home for a transformation in a wilderness of some kind.

One well-known Biblical hero was Jacob's son, Joseph, who was so favored and spoiled by his father that he caused jealousy among his older brothers. Joseph's departure from home is by his brother's selling him into Egyptian slavery where he will overcome his being spoiled through hardships in jail. But Joseph had a gift of interpreting dreams (he is a dreamer) and not only foresees the future famine but how to save ahead to divert this famine. The provision that Egypt has then attracts his brothers and Joseph, after some anger and testing, is able to rise above his negativity to forgive his brothers and heal the grief of his father who thought him dead. Although it sounds like the Hebrews are in a better place with a relative in authority, Joseph died and there came a pharaoh who "knew not Joseph" and who made the Israelites slaves setting the stage for the next major hero, Moses who would transform an entire tribe from out of Egypt into the wilderness.

At the folk level, Jung found a different kind of hero in Pinocchio. Pinocchio was a puppet, not a true boy, but he could move without strings. Pinocchio is not yet a moral personality but he has freedom along with some consequences. When he lies his nose grows long and he must tell the truth for it to decrease. He does have a conscience in the form of a cricket that is not integrated to Pinocchio's pride or pleasure seeking. The pride of his freedom leads him to a bad boys' runaway place where he smokes, drinks and eats all the bad food he wants. Pinocchio begins to resemble a donkey with ears and a tail and is headed for captivity where boys become donkey workers. Pinocchio tries to return home but his father has gone seeking him on a boat that ends up inside a whale. Out of sacrificial love, Pinocchio throws himself into the ocean and eventually finds his father inside the whale where he saves his father while almost losing his own life. His father prays as he had prayed in the beginning for a real boy. In response, a fairy godmother had described the three virtues needed for Pinocchio to become a "real boy". Now the fairy godmother confirms that Pinocchio has shown these three virtues: a/ honesty (no more lying), b/ selfless love, and c/ courage (to risk his life). He now becomes the flesh and blood son for which his father had prayed. He had to get through the shadow sides of his pride and pleasure seeking to find out who he was and then he could change from a shallow, fragmented puppet into an integrated whole self, of a Christ-self with more virtues than vices presenting a "morality play" for children (of all ages).

5.4—Jungian Campbell's Many Hero-type Initiations by Trial

Joseph Campbell, A Jungian disciple, has written about an archetypal hero (with 1,000 faces) who has to leave safety to explore the wilderness, go through ordeals to achieve an initiation into higher knowledge which is brought back to contribute to the civilized world (**Hero with A 1,000 Faces**).

Campbell explores the theory that important myths from around the world all share the following structure. A hero ventures forth from the world of common day into a region of supernatural wonder, fabulous forces are there encountered and a decisive victory is won, and the hero comes back from this mysterious adventure with the power to bestow boons on his fellow man. [Campbell, p.3]

The hero starts in the ordinary world but receives a call to enter an unusual world of strange powers and events. If the hero accepts the call to enter this strange world, the hero must face tasks which he may have to face alone or with assistance. If the hero survives, he may achieve a great gift such as the discovery of important self-knowledge. If the hero *is successful in returning, the gift he discovers may be used to improve the world.*

These three stages are often seen as Departure, Initiation and Return.

Departure begins with the hero venturing forth on the quest, Initiation describes the hero's various adventures along the way, and Return shows the hero's return home with knowledge and powers acquired on the journey.

The classic examples of Campbell's three part structure apply to the major founders of the world religions: Buddha, Moses, Jesus (and others) but also folk heroes like Pinocchio or Dorothy in **The Wizard of Oz.** *Campbell has discovered the structure of the hero's journey by using a mixture of Jungian archetypes, unconscious forces, and van Gennep's rites of passage rituals.*

5.5—Moses as a Hero and Symbol of Liberation from Addictions

Moses could have been set for life as a future pharaoh until he discovered that he was part of the Jewish slave caste working in the brick pits (literally pits). Moses lost everything of rank, privilege, power to become a slave. Once Moses killed a guard to stop him from abusing a fellow Jew, he was forced to go in exile in the wilderness to save himself. Moses received the call, not just to save himself, but to save his people on the Peaks of Mount Sinai. This "Peak experience" gave him a daunting challenge involving many pits (plagues) both for himself and the Egyptians until the Pharaoh finally "bottomed out" with the death of his son to allow the Hebrews to become free and journey into the wilderness in pursuit of a "promised land".

The heroic initiation of Moses is also a prototype of both addition recovery and relapse. Moses connected with his higher power, surrendered in obedience to the specifics (laws) of God's will and thus was an instrument for the liberation of an entire nation from the bondage of slavery (symbol of the bondage of addictions, sin). By contrast, Pharaoh did not learn humility and surrender until he "bottomed out" but he soon relapsed and reversed his liberation agreement sending his armies to recapture his slaves.

The liberation from alcohol or drug addition of the AA **recovery program has** 12 steps to freedom. Consider below the first six with their search for an unknown "god" or "higher power" needed when we find ourselves powerless in our lives.

1. We admitted we were powerless over our addiction because-our lives had become unmanageable.
2. Came to believe that a power greater than ourselves could restore us to sanity.
3. Made a decision to turn our will and our lives over to the care of God as we understood Him.
4. Made a searching and fearless moral inventory of ourselves.
5. Admitted to God, to ourselves, and to another human being the exact nature of our wrongs.
6. Were entirely ready to have God remove all these defects of character.

People lose their jobs, relationships, homes, and end up homeless due to their addiction to alcohol. Recently one of my students told her story wherein she lost all of the above, finally went to the 12 step program, became clean and sober to return to college and a home. Consider the character virtues and vices of the 9 different character types of the Enneagram as it appears in the next chapter (6).

Science can give us the facts about every peak and pit of our life's journey but these facts require our own personal philosophy of life to find the courage to face the challenges and the overview that reveals the value and meaning of both the pits and the peaks. Our civilization has given us a wisdom tradition for us to draw on lest we have to invent the wheel again and again. The current low ceiling and elitism of our secular techno-age has also cut us off from the transcendent revelations beyond suffering and death into a higher order of meaning and purpose. The common ground of both science and religion is the philosophical method that provides a context for evaluating how people's lives are transformed from the bondage of addition into freedom.

Young people in our secular culture think that "if there is no God, then everything is allowed." No accountability, no guilt, no raining on my hedonistic pursuit of the young liberated life style of drugs, alcohol, sex, *doing what feels good, being real and authentic without repression. Once someone faces the serious addiction of a friend or family member, the consolation of freedom at the expense of integrity is empty and hollow. The same is true for experiencing the death of a loved one up close. But we have a hope that the sages of our wisdom traditions have given us TRUTH to fill this void which our secular culture has allowed.*

CHAPTER SIX

POWER VS LOVE IN THE ENNEAGRAM'S PITS AND PEAKS

6.1—The Strengths and Weaknesses of Nine Enneagram Types

As we seek to identify points of stability in our life journey, we realize that personality is a relatively lasting point of continuity over the course of a lifetime along with career and marriage. We all pass through the eight stages outlined by Erikson but our personalities (and characters) make our journeys different.

The most common approaches to personality begin with temperament which show that there is a base line for spectrum of positive vs negatively oriented personalities and we tend to go back to that base line in response to either the peaks or pits of experience. Quite apart from our life experiences (such as secure attachment), it looks that our genes and biology may tilt some to unhappy feelings and others to the sunny side of life. All the more reason for spiritual fitness heroism with the unfairness of life. Aristotle, who was both a great philosopher and biologist, noted that happiness (the subjective sense of wellbeing) is more likely for those who are healthy, wealthy and wise (intelligent) so that they may achieve that level of excellence in their lives that is the full expression of their talents and uniqueness.

The Enneagram is ancient and precedes modern psychology but is consistent with Adler's view of competition in the "family constellation" to achieve love and power among siblings. The first born is going to be superior in his achievements to the next child younger by some years. Nevertheless, the first born feels "dethroned" as the only child and put out of the limelight as the baby requires attention and is loved without having to perform but just for being the last baby. In Adler's case, the first born child got even for being dethroned by making Alfred feel inferior in academics, sports and power. So we have noted that some of the Enneagram character types are all about establishing superiority and success while other character types are not competitive and may want to avoid conflict, such as the peacemaker or helper who could be the second born kids (the babies to the first borns).

As we survey, the different Enneagram types, we become aware that every one of the nine types has both peaks of virtue and pits of vice and the middle path is about the one compensating for the other to find balance. Yet all of these types can be in a highly functional state, a poorly dysfunctional state and some spectrum in-between. None of them by themselves are psychologically pathological though any of them can suffer from grief, depression, trauma, anxiety, or issues in anger management as they achieve or fail to achieve life span goals in timely ways.

6.2—The Peaks and Pits of the Three Power/Control Types (#1, 3, 8)

The peak (positive) sides of **Perfectionists** (#1) are that they are "ethical, reliable, productive, wise, idealistic, fair, honest, orderly, self-disciplined". All of these sounds great, but perfectionists have a pit side.

The negative (pit) sides of perfectionists are that they are "judgmental, inflexible, dogmatic, obsessive-compulsive, critical of others, overly serious, controlling, anxious, and jealous". (Baron, p.) Imagine this as your spouse or your boss and what would be some issues for you? Can you imagine being made to feel inferior and judged as inadequate? Perfectionists are typically first born.

But what is it like from the inside being a perfectionist. What do they like and what do they find difficult? **Perfectionists like** the self-discipline for accomplishments while keeping high standards and ethics. They like being the best that they can be to set a high standard for others. (Baron, p.13)

What's hard about being a Perfectionist is being disappointed with themselves when their high expectations are not met, that no matter what they do is never good enough. They never feel appreciated for their extra effort. Always trying to be a perfect employee, perfect wife, perfect mom is stressful. (Ibid. p14)

The **Achiever (#3)** is another competitive type but more interested in success than the ideals of the perfectionist. The peak (good) sides of the Achievers include optimism, confidence, industry, efficiency, self-propelled energy and practicality but the downsides include deception, narcissism, pretentiousness, vanity, superficiality, vindictiveness and their tendency to be overly competitive.(Ibid.) The Perfectionist will win but only on the high ground while the Achiever's motto seems to be "Just win, baby, win" (Al Davis of the Raiders). The balance of the two sides keeps the Achiever healthy but the unchecked narcissism could take them into dysfunction of a personality disorder (Narcissistic self-centered) Extraverted Achievers may do well in Sales or in the entertainment industry where either wealth or fame are the payoffs.)

What's **to like** about being an **Achiever** (#3) is"being optimistic, friendly, upbeat and providing well for his family, recovering quickly from setbacks, being competent and informed, working efficiently. (Ibid., p. 42). What's **hard** about being an Achiever is "having to put up with the inefficiency and incompetence of others while always being "on" with the fear of not being seen as successful and having to put on facades to impress people to hang on to feeling successful. (Ibid. p42) One can imagine that the Achiever would like these strengths, but only from the inside do we realize the price of keeping up one's image.

The third type of first born driven to excel is the **Asserter (#8)** who has a strong will and a need to control. The assets of Asserters are that they are "direct, authoritative, loyal, energetic, earthy, protective, and self-confident". Whereas their downside is that Asserters tend to be "controlling, rebellious, insensitive, domineering, self-centered, skeptical, and aggressive." (ibid.) Such personalities would do well as executives, chairmen, political leaders, and heads of business organizations. In marriage relationships, two Asserters would make for a conflictual pattern unless adjustments were made. Often leaders and followers connect up in a marriage to avoid ongoing power struggles.

*What does the Asserter find positive (peaks) about their personality type? The **Asserter (#8)** likes "being in charge and meeting challenges head on which means being courageous, straightforward and honest, independent and self-reliant. They like protecting and supporting those close to them and upholding just causes. They also like getting all the enjoyment that they can out of life which means that they both work hard and play hard. (Ibid. 110)*

*What's **hard** (pits) about being an Asserter is that they sometimes overwhelm people with their bluntness and scare them away without meaning to. They tend to get impatient with other's incompetence and can get high blood pressure when things don't go right. They tend to put too much pressure on themselves, stick their necks out for others, get no appreciation and then have a hard time forgetting injuries or injustices." (Ibid. p 110)*

It is not difficult to see how each of these three competitive types could excel at work when they find the right match of their skills, passions, ideals with the right organization and product or service. More challenging would be marriage relationships where the ideal is mutuality in power sharing and reciprocity of needs being met. For the woman, transparent communication of vulnerable feelings is an important engagement that leads to the fulfillment (peak) of intimacy.

A man who is too caught up with being in control and superior would find the humility and transparency of marital communication difficult. What are three of the non-competitive personality types most often related to the later children in the family (last born or middle positions) who tend toward the inferiority complex in contrast to the superiority complex of the competitive types?

6.3—The Peaks and the Pits of Three Non-competitive Types (#2, 4, 6, 9)

Three other personality types seek to avoid competition and conflict: the helper (#2), the peacemaker (#9), and the loyal skeptic (#6).

*The **Helpers (#2)** at their best (peak) are "loving, caring, adaptable, insightful, generous, enthusiastic, tuned in to how people feel". No doubt all of these qualities make them good caretakers, but there is a related problematic side. At their worst (pit side), the **Helper** is martyr-like,* indirect, manipulative, possessive, hysterical, overly accommodating, overly demonstrative". (Ibid.) The Helper seem love-oriented but the love is imbalanced toward the other with an incomplete self love which allows reciprocity of both power and caregiving.

These negative qualities keep the Helper types from being a true giver because they expect to be appreciated for the giving and can be very hurt when they are taken for granted which they often are. Then some passive aggressive playing the martyr (poor me) or indirect barbs might fly. When the two sides compensate each other with some integration, serious problems are avoided but in a dysfunctional family relationship, the Helpers can be the enablers for alcohol or drug addicts, can't set limits and say "no" to children and can raise brats due to their wanting to please and inability to confront straight up. The profession of therapy attracts people of this character type where empathy and caring are easy but setting limits and confrontation are more difficult to which the writer can affirm.

What's to **like** (peaks) about being a **Caretaker/Helper (#2) is** being able make friends "by knowing what people need and helping" by being warm, caring, generous, sensitive as well as enthusiastic and fun-loving". (Ibid, p28).

What's **hard** (pits) about being a Caretaker is "not being able to say 'no', set limits or express real feelings resulting in low self-esteem and feeling drained from overdoing for others. Their fear of being selfish makes them not do things for themselves but then they are disappointed and resentful when their care- taking is not reciprocated, (Ibid. p28) This additional information is helpful in getting a fuller picture of the Helper but it is consistent with what one would expect.

A second non-competitive type is the **Peacemaker (#9)** who is "pleasant, peaceful, generous, patient, receptive, diplomatic, open-minded, and empathic" (Ibid.) and could be a good balance for an Asserter at work or in a marriage (peak side).

Like everyone else, the peacemaker has a down pit side. At their worst, peacemakers are: spaced-out, forgetful, stubborn, obsessive, apathetic, passive-aggressive, judgmental, and unassertive". To avoid passive aggression and achieve equity, a marriage between the #8 and the #9 would need the Peacemaker to learn assertiveness and the Asserter would need to learn to share power and control in areas less essential to their wellbeing. How does the peacemaker see their own peaks and pits relative to their own happiness striving?

What **Peacemakers (#9)** like (peaks) about being one is that they can go with the flow, are able to relax to have a good time while being non-judgmental and accepting. They like caring for others, and knowing that most people enjoy their easy going personalities. They see many different sides of an issue which makes them good mediators. (Ibid. p122)

What's hard (pits) about being a peacemaker is that they care too much about what others think of them, too sensitive to criticism that they take personally. They don't like being judged for being indecisive or placid or for being confused about what they really want because they are already critical of themselves for not taking more initiative and having more discipline." (Ibid. p122)

The third non-competitive type is the Loyal Skeptics (#6) whose peak virtues are "loyal, likable, caring, warm, compassionate, witty, practical, helpful, and responsible". On the negative (pit) side, this character type tends to be "hyper-vigilant, controlling, unpredictable, judgmental, paranoid, defensive, rigid, self-defeating, and testy." (ibid.)

What to like about being a Loyal Skeptic (#6) is "being committed and faithful to family and friends, being responsible, hardworking and compassionate toward others, and being smart.

The Loyal Skeptic has a positive side that fights fear, likes confronting danger bravely, being direct and assertive and being a non-conformist." (Ibid. p. 84)

What's hard about being a Loyal skeptic is the "constant pro/ con involved in trying to make up their minds and procrastinating for fear of failure with self-confidence lacking. They become exhausted from worrying, scanning for danger, to being self-critical. (Ibid. p84)

6.4—The Individualist Pursuit of Empowered Self-love Happiness (#4,5, 7)

A more introverted creative type than the achiever is the Romantic (#4) who are warm, compassionate, introspective, creative, intuitive, supportive and refined on the upside. The downside of Romantics is that they get depressed, self-conscious, guilt-ridden, moralistic, withdrawn, stubborn, moody, and self-absorbed". (Ibid.) A writer tends to be of this ilk and is wonderful to be around when creative but may be moody, self-absorbed and depressed when he has writer's block and the creative juice are not flowing. The connections between character types and careers apply to both my trades as therapist and writer and both the virtues and vices do appear with some relevance. Please continue to try these character types to see your happiness goals and the built in frustrations from the personality side.

Another introvert unlikely to be the first born is the Observer (#5 who has the virtues of being analytical, persevering, sensitive, wise, objective, perceptive, and self-contained along with the vices of being intellectually arrogant, stingy, stubborn, distant, critical of others, unassertive, and negative. (Ibid). Observers would do well in academic careers or careers in financial planning but might be the "Avoider" in a marital relationship using their intellect as a defense against that part of emotional intimacy that is ego wounding or humbling. Parents can often see this dynamic with a son-in-law but it would be important to notice the roles and dynamics of both partners.

Adventurers (#7) are very easy to identify because they are fun-loving, spontaneous, imaginative, productive, enthusiastic, quick, confident, charming and curious. What you don't notice until you are in a close relationship with them is that they can be narcissistic, impulsive, unfocused, rebellious, undisciplined, possessive, manic, self-destructive, restless and definitely intolerant of boredom". (Ibid.) We have a family member who fits this description on the good sides and we were surprised that she copped to much the other side as well. Nobody is all the categories but with the things that do apply, you can fill out the rest and get a concept of how the person is motivated.

6.5—What the Individualist Types Likes and Finds Hard

We can each imagine what each of us would like or dislike since every type has a mix of virtue and vice, but how does each type identify for them what is most liked and most difficult. See if there are any surprises.

What's to like about being a Romantic (#4) is making warm connections with people through empathy and a sense of humor while being seen as unique in creativity. They like being intuitive and finding a deeper meaning in life through beauty and truth.

What's hard about being a Romantic is "expecting too much from life and longing for what they don't have so that they experience dark moods of emptiness and despair. When they expect too much of themselves, they have feelings of self-hatred and shame feeling unloveable. (Ibid.)

What's to like about being an Observer #5) is "standing up and viewing life objectively until coming to a thorough understanding of causes and effects. They like being able to do what they think is right without being influenced by social pressures and consider this integrity.

Observers like being calm during crises and not being caught up with material possessions and status seeking." (Ibid. 72) What's hard about being an observer is "being slow to put their knowledge and insights into the world due to trouble with succinct communication. Observers feel resentful that those with better social skills with less intelligence do better than them. Observers try to avoid social pressures and feel bad when they see themselves acting like a "know-it-all" defensively.

What's to like about being an Adventurer (#7) is "always being optimistic and not letting life's troubles get them down. They like being spontaneous and free-spirited, having "the guts" to take risks to try exciting adventures and being outspoken and outrageous as part of the fun. They like their variety of interests, their being generous and trying to make the world a better place." (Ibid. p98) What's hard about being an Adventurer is "not having enough time to do all the things that they want to do and not completing the things that they start. As "jacks of all trades" they don't benefit by specializing to advance their careers. They can get ungrounded and lost between plans and fantasies. (Ibid. 98)

From these more subjective self revelations, we find ourselves more sympathetic to these external behaviors which can be off-putting or defensive. We understand the turmoil the Questioner goes through staying loyal and yet asking necessary questions whose answers can change one's allegiance. We see how the Perfectionist is just as critical and demanding of themselves as they are of others for whom they hold responsibility (employees, spouses, children). The Asserter is demanding but also protecting of loved one. Each type has their own demons with which to wrestle and the fact of the battle they all share though each a different type of battle for truth and identity with self-esteem.

6.6—Happiness Goals and Gaps for Each of the Nine Types

The happiness goals of each of the lifestyles are evident from their titles which are primary to the identity of each as to love, power, happiness.

1/ to be as perfect as possible (through power),
2/ to be helpful and take care of others (for love)
3/ to achieve success (power) and to be admired (earned love)
4/ to be creative and have warm relationships (love)
5/ to observe first without social pressures and only then to act (delayed power and delayed love)
6/ to be loyal to family/friends (love) but also ask probing questions (the power of confrontation for truth)
7/ to enjoy the fun of adventures with variety that avoids boredom (the love of autonomy/power, and the self-nurturing of fun)
8/ being assertive to get needs met (power) and protect loved one,
9/ to keep peace and help settle conflicts both within and without (the love of harmony, unity at the price of power).

In general, the personalities are suited for these happiness goals which developed originally in the context of their family constellations when they were children and exported to new and quasi-families. It would appear that these personalities remain intact because they are socially reinforced in positive ways more than in the negative. Nevertheless, there are "happiness gaps" for each lifestyle because the world as a whole is not perfect, not fair, not equal, not balanced. Often the conflict comes from within the personality itself, perhaps the negative side to a good thing or a good thing taken too far or not far enough.

6.7—Issues in Integrity for Each of the Nine Types

Three of these nine types have issues with **anger** *and deal with anger differently. Asserters aren't afraid to express their anger directly but can offend people if they lack tact. Perfectionists see anger as a character flaw and try to hold it back or hide it which makes them defensive. Peacemakers can become out of touch with angry emotions. Peacemakers* need to heed the commonsense warning that "what you don't own (admit) can own (control) you."

Three others have issues with fear and cope with fears differently. Observers find safety in knowledge but intellectualism can become a defense that cuts them off from their feelings. Questioners find relief from fear with getting the approval of authority figures or in rebelling against them (two opposite movements) both of which may undermine the value they hold for genuine loyalty. The Adventurer is afraid of having unpleasant negative emotions and distracts themselves with activities which improve their moods but leave their problems still unresolved.

Finally, three are concerned about presenting images. The Helper wants a loving image but can't integrate the "tough love" that sets the limits and assertiveness they need for balance. Romantics want to be seen as creative and original, and suffer as they struggle to achieve these goals. Achievers want to be seen as successful and as winners, and find the inevitable losses and failures intolerable. (Ibid. p6)

For the perfectionist, the challenge of doing things right is not being too angry at those who don't get it right or too self-critical For the helper the challenge is not being resentful when they are not appreciated which means that they must be less attached to their giving. The challenge of happiness for the achiever is honesty instead of image-making when success fall short. The challenge of happiness for the creative romantic is accepting the price of the "labor pains" which creativity requires and not inflict the misery of their "stuck places" on others. The observer's happiness is knowing everything by first observing long but they must deal with the slowness and inactivity that this observing involves. The Questioner's happiness is having security and permission to ask questions and change their minds but they have to deal with the guilt of being disloyal. The Adventurer's happiness is having the fun of adventures but this mode of life can make them unreliable unless they learn more tolerance of boredom and less addiction to fun. The Asserter's happiness comes from always being strong and self sufficient but they must sacrifice domination and autonomy for the interdependency and mutuality of marriage. as well as the give and take of teamwork in their careers. The Peacemaker's happiness is being able to keep peace by avoiding conflict but sometimes the peace and harmony must be sacrificed to get to a deeper truth and this can be hard for a Peacemaker. In short, all of the Enneagrams have happiness gaps which require courage, sacrifice, understanding and/or humility to achieve. All of these virtues are components of integrity and heroism. The inability to admit both the strengths and the weakness of each Enneagram can result in pursuing a false happiness and a false identity as discovered by Karen Horney in her clinical work.

6.8— Horney's Critique of Personalities Lacking Wholeness

Horney provides strong motivation for each character type on the Enneagram to admit and affirm both their strengths and weaknesses and to build their identity on a positive, realistic synthesis of the two. For Horney, denial of our inner human condition leads to a false self. Self-realization comes from embracing both our inferiority and our superiority in honesty. The false self pretends to be only what is superior and strong and denies what is inferior and weak but this self becomes contrived. The false self strives for self-glory and keeping up false social image. Only the true self can be genuine, spontaneous, honest and real. True intimacy requires the courage of self-disclosure, sharing with your mate times of failings, fears, shame, guilt, weakness. The male ego is threatened by such vulnerability, but time has shown women to be the better source of support than men because they self-disclose, can cry together, can be angry at each other, can apologize and get even closer.

Women are men's guides to greater emotional truth and closeness and essential sources of bonding for children. Only a woman would understand the truth that "healthy friction" in family life is a requirement for "self-actualization". The home must be a safe place for the whole range of human feelings to be felt, expressed, understood and accepted if we are to become whole and authentic.

Karen Horney was the earliest female to challenge Freud's ideas and like Adler had to "take the highway" to find her own way. Karen Horney had the courage to challenge Freud's chauvinism. Women did not have "penis envy", they had power envy for what the penis symbolized as much as men had "womb envy" for being unable to give birth to a baby.

Freud's position with his clients was to be in the superior position as the doctor who would be the expert on the matter of interpreting the content of the client's dreams or the dynamics of the client's transference behaviors. Horney and Adler sought an equalitarian relationship with clients. The therapists had the outside perspective informed by theory but the clients had the inside subjective reality, Therapist and client formed an interdependent twosome team, both with knowledge gaps. Feminism finds equalitarian roles more supportive of our humanity while hierarchical roles are full of power inequalities that are problematic.

Horney followed Adler's idea of lifestyle patterns set up by the dynamics of the family of origin which could become neurotic. Adler focused on sibling rivalry coming from the superior firstborn being "dethroned" by the forever lovable baby with no need to prove anything. If parents played into this love contest with their own favoritism, the issue would be internalized and go on forever. Horney looked more to the parents role in establishing the proper nurturing climate for children.

Horney noted three neurotic types are driven out of neediness. The first needs boundaries and assertiveness to be authentically loving. The last is power driven and needs to learn reciprocity. The middle seems to avoid the contests both of love and power to develop their own inner self love and autonomy. Different kinds of half steps of love and power.

6.9—The Subjective View of Love and Power in Personality Types

What are the strengths (peaks) and weaknesses (pits) in your personality lifestyle? For the writer/therapist the helper, peace-maker and relational pleaser come up meaning the feared pit is anger and conflict. Marriage has helped me to safely deal with my anger past the passive aggressive into more assertive to be increase my power and my tendency to be a listener has helped build communication skills for intimacy (love) with the two together being a middle path out of an original inferiority into feeling good enough in the "work" or marriage and parenting in the give and take of the roles of power within both. The parenting style tends toward the counselor (hearing feelings) but the coach style of warmth but high expectations is a better style according to research. I encourage the reader for their entries here on personality strengths and weaknesses thorough peaks and pits of roles in marriage and parenting.

The ongoing first question for the personal sharing by the reader is a general question of truth. What of this chapter jumps out as being helpful (one concept of truth) and what is least helpful, questionable or confusing.

Our theory of truth contributes toward providing a series of holistic views of data which is truth from the top down. Other theories of truth prefer truth from the bottom up starting with solid empirical research that is built upon and critical of generalities.

One practical goal of this book is to stimulate the reader to make a biography of their own focused on love and power in the lifespan, marriage and family issues as influenced by personality types and questions on religion and the afterlife - all of which provide the basis for purpose and meaning in life and help the reader chart out his/ her own philosophy of life which secular society does not provide.

Clearly some character types are focused on power (success, excellence, control, performance) such as the Perfectionist, Achiever and Asserter. Freud dominated but at the price of losing the "love" (connection, respect, trust) of his most important early followers. Typically these power-driven types are first borns or following the role and script of the first born in a family.

Other character types seek to avoid the conflict of power struggles with some form of love. The Helper focuses on the other rather than the self and seeks to fulfill the needs of the other. The Peacemaker avoids conflicts by downsizing the sources of conflicts and pretending agreement. The Helper and Peacemaker version of "love" is forging a quick harmony by limiting areas of disagreement. Is this compromised (erstatz) version of love with a compromised truth? The true love of a marriage requires a reciprocal sharing both of power and of meeting needs (tangible and intangible"Love"). Attachment theory shows the marriage pattern distortions when reciprocity is lacking and one partner dominates and the other partner either avoids, becomes a victim, or compromises integrity by being a people-pleaser without authentic love or genuine conflict resolution.

CHAPTER SEVEN

POWER AND LOVE IN HAPPINESS RESEARCH

7.1—Aristotle's View of Happiness Virtue in Character

Aristotle defined happiness as "flourishing or wellbeing" seen as an end in itself rather than a means to another source of fulfillment and as such has a measure of stability.

Aristotle believed that some external goods (e.g., life and health) were necessary preconditions for happiness and that others (such as wealth, friends, fame, honor) were "embellishments" to fill out a good life for a virtuous person, but that the exercise of virtue was the core constitutive element of happiness. The virtuous person alone can attain happiness without being miserable even in the face of misfortune. Happiness combines an element over which we have greater control (virtue) with elements over which we have lesser control (health, wealth, friends).

Virtues are habits of the soul which express right reason acquired by both practice and habit. Virtue is a repeated pattern of right actions, but virtue is difficult to attain because our natural inclinations often lead us astray. Since our immature state can be destructive, a good upbringing is essential to develop habits both of right thinking and right (moral) action. In most cases, a virtue will fall between two vices, one representing an excess of a certain passion and the other representing a defect.

Virtue is finding the golden mean of moderation (the middle path) in both external goods and social life. Frugality is the right use of money that avoids the extremes of either being too stingy or too extravagant. Courage is the middle path that moderates between cowardice and unnecessary risk-taking. Virtue avoids the extremes while finding the benefits of opposite sides.

7.2—The Current Support for Happiness as an "Inside Job"

Current happiness research supports Aristotle's view that external circumstances are not the cause of lasting happiness. Money does not appear to buy happiness. A large raise brings happiness in the short run but it would only be a matter of time before your expectations change to fit your new budget so that you're just as happy as you were before the raise! This holds true for new houses, new cars, new gadgets, and all of the other material goods that people spend so much time pining for.

Current research suggests that happiness is a combination of how satisfied you are with your life (for example, finding meaning in your work) and how good you feel on a day-to- day basis. Both of these are only relatively stable—that is, our life changes, and our mood fluctuates. (Acacia Parks, 1/8/15). The lifelong systems of work and family are satisfying (right fit career and right fit mate but we do not choose our kids and those who struggle long into adulthood impact the midlife parents who otherwise have a stability in career and mate adjustments. Health is another big matter needing habits toward physical fitness but with the impact of genes still beyond our control and quite impacting requiring a measure of heroic spiritual fitness.

The distribution of happiness is not really fair. Consistent research show that people are born with a certain happiness "set point" to which they return after the short term impact of circumstances settle down. Genetic set point is virtually half of the cause of feelings of happiness. Those tilted toward depression and/or anxiety have an heroic challenge to pursue their happiness goals.

More strange still, if you can believe this, only 10% of lasting happiness due to life circumstances as long as we are not in dire straits and our basic needs are being met. We gain and lose jobs, have gains and losses in possessions and income and we bounce back to our set point sooner than later. So what is the cause of the remaining 40%? The researchers tell has that almost half the cause of happiness is "an inside job" of our attitudes, beliefs, value systems, personal meaning in life and so on. In short, happiness is a matter of heroic choices as a habit. Choosing to appreciate and anticipate goodness along with the attitude of gratitude create the power of positive thinking that brings about a positive lifestyle. By looking at the glass half full instead of half empty and loving life despite its imperfections, we are empowered to fight depression, stress and low self esteem. Basking in our bank of happy memories (rather than marinating in regrets) buoys us up as we savor past joys that we believe will come again.

Our thesis on happiness is consistent with Freud's beliefs that work and love are the two pillars of happiness, especially in a right fit lasting career and marriage/family. The happiness research supports these two area albeit with some qualifications.

7.3—The Love Power of a Right Fit Sustained Marriage

A quarter of today's young adults will have never married by 2030 and both remaining unmarried and divorcing are more common among less-educated, lower-income people. Educated, high-income people still marry at high rates and are less likely to divorce. Recent research indicates that being married makes people happier and more satisfied with their lives than those who remain single – particularly during the most stressful periods, like midlife crises.

In all but a few parts of the world, even when controlling for people's life satisfaction before marriage, being married made them happier. Researchers found that the benefits of marriage persist when there is a close friendship within marriage. Those who consider their spouse or partner to be their best friend get about twice as much life satisfaction from marriage as others, the study found.

Marriage has undergone a drastic shift in the last half century. In the past, marriage was utilitarian wherein women looked for a husband to make money and men looked for a woman to manage the household. In recent decades, the roles of men and women have become more similar. As a result, spouses have taken on roles as companions and confidants, particularly those who are financially stable. The benefits of marital *friendship are most vivid during midlife when people tend to experience a dip in life satisfaction. People who are married can handle midlife stress better than those who aren't because they have a shared load and shared friendship," (Helliwell)*

Overall, the research comes to a largely optimistic conclusion. People have the capacity to increase their happiness levels and avoid falling deep into midlife crisis by finding support in long-term relationships.

7.4—Pursuing Happiness Through the Power of Work

From a classic study on work by Studs Terkel, it is clear that work in the economy has been marked by more pits than peaks. Terkel found the "happy few" who savored their daily jobs. The piano tuner finds the sound that delights. The stonemason is satisfied with a job well done independent of his paycheck.

Terkel says that "jobs are too small for our spirits". We need a calling, a vocation (Terk, xxiv). What is the calling that work represents? A call to find dignity and social esteem, a call to find some purpose and meaning in life. a call to manifest our hidden talents for the benefit of our human community?

In his book, Working, Studs Terkel wrote almost 600 pages based on interviews from every walk of life. The recurrent message that Terkel heard was "discontent". Typically there is not the "good fit" which allows the worker to use his talents to benefit society and be paid accordingly. 'I'm a machine' says the spot welder. "I'm caged" says the bank teller and hotel clerk. The complaints of blue collar workers are echoed by white collar employees in the phase: "I'm a robot" from the young accountant to the receptionist to migrant worker. Terkel tries to get to the heart of the problem.

The automated pace of our daily jobs wipe out name, face and feeling and make people question the work ethic with absenteeism according to Terkel's findings. Craftsmanship is no longer valued and is replaced with slovenly work. Nevertheless, there was a search for meaning at work, a desire to "be remembered". Therefore, the aging waitress fights humiliation (and her arthritis) by "setting tables like a ballerina." "When I put the plate down, you don't hear a sound. When I pick up a glass, I want it to be just right." (Terk, xii)

Along with the search for meaning at work, there is a search for dignity. Titles give dignity. The janitor is "the building engineer", the salesman is "an account executive", the copy chief is a vice president (like most of the company) and the garbage man is "the sanitary engineer". There is the fear of no longer being needed in a world of needless things which make work surreal and unnatural. A prior job of "putting numbers on a paper" did not feel real to someone who became a fireman. "Putting out a fire and giving mouth-to-mouth to someone dying, that's real." (Ibid.)

For many, the story of work is a story of violence to the spirit as well as to the body with nervous breakdowns and daily humiliations. "Many are the walking wounded whose achievement is to get through the day." (Ibid.)

Marx put blame for the dehumanization of work on the industrial revolution. Craftsmen would create a useful work of art from start to finish and take satisfaction in its creation. In the factory system, each person installs only one part and feels little connection to the finished airplane, car or ship when thousands of parts were installed by others. City dwellers do not have the satisfaction of producing their own food from their gardens and farms.

To paraphrase Eleanor Roosevelt, we are all like tea bags who only find their full strength when we are "in hot water", we grow to maturity by facing crises (Erikson), and we are "transformed by trouble" (R. Warren). When trouble abounds, grace abounds more if only we can bypass the pride that causes us to hide. The virtues of humility and honest transparency before God liberate us from the prison of pride to enter into daily, loving fellowship in trusting confidence. There is such great need in the world from homelessness to prisons that deform more than transform. Could our call be found in finding empathy for some segment of this hurting world?

Living from the center of our souls is a life that integrates every opposite into a reconciling balance. We work with efficient habits but we yield to God's grace. We fulfill our individual purpose but may be called to sacrifice at any point to serve the communal good or God's call for this moment. Living the resurrected life gives us faith that overcomes death without denying its destructive power. Amidst all the troubles, there is a recurrent, victorious joy that allows us to talk about the possibility of an abiding happiness in a world of troubles.

On the other side, work can be a source of joy, triumph and fulfillment of using one's talents well for to profit both the worker's needs and the greater good of society. Consider the following celebration about the glory and power of work by Angela Morgan: "Work! Thank God for the might of it, the ardor, the urge the delight of it - Work that springs from the heart's desire setting the brain and the soul on fire. What's so good as the heat of it, the beat of it, the command of it challenging brain, heart and hand. (Eng,'79)"

7.5—Happiness as a Choice Despite Circumstances

The vast current research on happiness agrees that happiness is largely "an inside job".(Powell) but one of the most surprising findings is the role of attitude and choice that can be made despite negative circumstances. This little vignette provides an extraordinary example of heroic attitude over what appears a happiness pit.

Mr. Jones was a 92-year-old legally blind man who was just being moved to a nursing home after the recent passing of his wife of 70 years. As Mr. Jones' caregiver described his new room, Mr. Jones said with enthusiasm, "I love it". When Mr. Jones was cautioned to wait until he got into the room, Mr. Jones described his belief that happiness is a decision.

"Happiness is something you decide on ahead of time. Whether I like my room or not doesn't depend on how the furniture is arranged, it's how I arrange my mind. I already decided to love it." Mr. Jones went on to explain how happiness is a decision that he has to make every morning when he first wakes up. "I have a choice; I can spend the day in bed recounting the difficulty I have with the parts of my body that no longer work, or get out of bed and be thankful for the ones that do.

Mr. Jones explained that he has stored up all the happy memories just for his hard times. Jones sees old age as a "bank account" from which he can withdraw from what he has deposited. ("Happiness Decisions")

The "Serenity Prayer" is a helpful and heroic guide to find the balance between acceptance and change in difficult circumstances. "Lord, give me the courage to change the things I can change, the serenity to accept the things I cannot change, and the Wisdom to know the difference."

7.6—The Power of Love to Embrace all Opposites

Og Mandino was a salesman in the market place who discovered success at work through the activity of love. He allowed the power of his positive thinking in love to embrace every opposite, showing always the glass half full in all circumstances.

> "I will greet this day with love in my heart. And how will I do this? I will love the sun for it warms my bones, yet I will love the rain for it cleanses my spirit. I will love the light for it shows the way, yet I will love the darkness for it shows me the stars. I will welcome happiness for it enlarges my heart, yet I will endure sadness for it opens my soul...I will love all manner of men for each has qualities to be admired even if they be hidden (the rich, the poor, the young, the old).

Mandino showed a positive side or benefit for every seemingly negative person and his practice of this art in the market place. This love attracted business that makes him successful. Mandino silently says to each person he encounters in the market place "I love you" with an open heart and a determination to practice love for all mankind as an end in itself with success being the by-product rather than the goal.

Christians believe that when you feed the hungry or clothe the naked or give shelter to the homeless, you do it as if this person were the hidden Christ. Where our lesser self might bring distance from unattractive people with problems, believers see Christ who is suffering, as the least of these which includes those in prison or those dying in hospitals.

Perfection may be valid striving for certain character types, but one writer has found the "Gift of Imperfection" to be a source of balance and sanity.

7.7—The "Gifts of Imperfection" for the "Wholehearted Life"

The "pits" of imperfection have been found to hold "gifts" as we let go of the the perfectionist illusions of ourselves and "embrace who we really are" according to research by Brene Brown that parallels our conclusions.

The heights of perfectionism are illusory peaks of bondage and the hidden gifts of imperfection helps us into the middle path of "wholeheartedness" if we but humble ourselves and face our fears head on with "courage, compassion, and connection"

(B. Brown, The Gift of Imperfection. p.125). These three virtues were the antidotes to the pains of imperfection that Brown experienced: "fearful, judgmental and alone". (Ibid.)

Brown feared the disapproval and loss of self-esteem if people saw her vulnerabilities/imperfections until she realized that the greater danger was losing touch with her true "wholehearted" self with its mix of strengths and weaknesses.

Brown's sees perfectionism as a self destructive and addictive belief system that if I look perfect, I can avoid blame, judgment, shame. Perfectionism is other-focused: "What will they think?"

By contrast, Brown says that "To become fully human means... growing gentler toward human weakness, practicing forgiveness of failures to live up to divine standards...receiving the human condition as blessing and not curse, in all its achingly frail and redemptive reality."

According to Christian theologians, 'All virtues have the goal to enable humans to acts conducive to true happiness. Natural happiness is attainable by our human powers but supernatural happiness exceeds the capacity of unaided human nature. To attain the highest level of happiness, humans must be helped with supernatural powers of the theological virtues to enable them to attain their final destiny: faith, hope and love and the highest of these is love. These virtues describe the middle path avoiding the false peak of pride and investing in the lowliness of humility, self control, temperance, patience and so on.

7.8—Power and Love in Our Human Condition as "an Untidy Mess"

Charles Davis has presented an intriguing counterpoint to the happiness research in his article "No Key to Happiness" (NCR, 12/15/72, p.12) which has stuck with me for over some thirty years and is a fitting way to end our journey with open mindedness and wonder. Davis answers the question "is happiness possible in this imperfect world with our "human condition"?

"No, happiness is not available...life offers no one a stable, secure, rounded fulfillment. Life for the best of us is an untidy mess of unfinished business, broken achievements, personal failures, half successes, short-lived triumphs, belated insights, noble desires and shameful deeds. Perhaps we win praise for some successes, perhaps through the years, we accumulate a little wisdom and goodness, but life remains an incomplete and unsavory jumble."

Davis modifies his view of the pits of life as an "untidy mess with the qualification that there are "unexpected moments outside of our control" in which we are suddenly "filled and overwhelmed by what we have been seeking" and that there are even peak moments of "breathtaking perfection". Davis believes the pits of our "fragmentary and unstable achievements are what leave us open for the momentary "flashes of joy" (peaks) which become "vehicles carrying us to the transcendent" but only if we can let go and not try to possess them). (Ibid.).

Davis' description of a middle path between peaks and pits is critical of the happiness research that does not also include the requirement of spiritual transformation (fitness) in keeping with our thesis stressing the necessity of moral heroism mindful of "the untidy mess" of our human condition and our capabilities of manifesting both our higher and lower selves.

Secular sources do not have answers for the final pit of death or the "untidy mess" of short-lived triumphs and broken achievements so we must continue to seek on.

7.9—Power and Love in the Integration of "Spirituality" and Therapy

The "untidy mess" of life has led this author to seek meaning and healing in the integration of psychotherapy and spirituality as described by Corey.

Corey defines "Spirituality" as the movement toward "love, meaning, hope, transcendence, connectedness and compassion" including the development of a values system and the capacity for creativity." (Corey, p. 461). Research has shown that greater openness to the spiritual tends to bring a change in lifestyle beyond symptom relief. The role of the therapist is to help the client find their own pathway for spiritual fitness with openness and encouragement. The religious beliefs of clients need to be respected and understood from an holistic view.

Both spirituality and therapy seek self-understanding, self-acceptance, admission of one's shortcoming followed by self-forgiveness, dealing with guilt and then allowing forgiveness for others. (Corey, p. 462) Spirituality and therapy each give strength in critical times by finding purpose in life and learning to accept human imperfections. Both therapy and spirituality help the person answer the identity question of "who am I?" (Ibid.) Both seek to decrease blame and increase the taking of personal responsibility. Both seek to foster the development of the best self while accepting and integrating the lesser self. In seeking to overcome the addictions which block the best self, psychology has found the 12 step program helpful in transcending the limits of willpower and the ego.

The practice of psychotherapy has found that religious people find comfort, calm, hope and inspiration from their faith and as a group tend to be happier than those who are do not have any religious faith.

The bottom line of any research is its contribution to helping us find and live out our best selves. What are some simple lessons that help us live out from this map of our lifespan pursuit of happiness with balance? The combination of psychotherapy and the search for spiritual fitness guide us.

CHAPTER EIGHT

HAPPINESS THROUGH HEROIC VIRTUES: BALANCED RESILIENCE THROUGH LIFE'S PITS AND PEAKS

8.1—Resilience Through Life's Pits and Peaks

How do we humans find a stable pathway through changing ups (peaks) and downs (pits) of life? Life's pits can rob us of hope but holding on to an unbalanced solution through peaks experiences can lead to addictions rather than balanced fulfillments. We seek a freedom from the pit afflictions through the highs of alcohol, drugs, sex, food, control over others, and ego gratifications. Sadly, we end up stuck on ourselves (self-centeredness), on power, or on substances from food to drugs instead of the freedom to which our peaks experiences had drawn us. Even our highest longing for God in the peaks meets with the need to face the same ups and downs of our human condition. What is the answer to cope with the instability and disappointments of our lifespan's search for happiness through the ups and downs that are beyond our control? Perhaps we need to break our dilemma into two separate questions: how do we find resilience from the pits of life and how do we find stability through the changing ups and downs in our quest for a sustained happiness?

At the beginning of Western philosophy, Aristotle pointed to a "golden mean" balance which would provide moderation to all extremes. Aristotle saw value in both the pits and the peaks because both would require us to learn and practice "virtues" such as discipline and humility. Aristotle advocated a big picture perspective from a reliable peak vantage to provide a map of hope revealing peaks that would follow pits as well as the lessons learned from both extremes to provide a stability on a middle path which teach us the needed virtues for both the ups and downs of life.

Humans have peaks and pits within themselves which require the practice of virtue for resilience both within our human condition and the injustices or tragedies in the world itself. We would have to swim against the stream of our own pit forces to find the middle path of stability and truth. We would need to practice the relevant virtue to meet the current pit challenges for resilience, be it some variation of discipline or humility. Those who chose virtues over vices more often than not can be seen as "heroes" as they represent the sacrifices and courage required be part of the cosmic battle of good against evil. St. Thomas Aquinas would adopt the peak overview of Aristotle to give faces to the sources of good and evil as the cosmic battle of the kingdom of heaven versus the kingdom of hell as they are both represented on earth.

The big question is how do we find happiness given the pits and peaks of life? Our big answer is we overcome the instability of life's ups and downs through the heroic virtues which help us achieve the resilience to bounce up from the pits into the true peaks of life without getting seduced by the illusions and addictions of false peak solutions. An overview search of our lifespan experience shows seven life situations where resilience is required to overcome imbalances from pits and/or peaks. We begin with an overview (1), end with our conclusions (9) like the two slices of our sandwich with the meat and cheese inside as follows:

1- An _overview_ on how resilience helps lifespan problems of peaks & pits.
2- Issues with peaks & pits in _Marriage._
3- The challenges of peaks & pits within our _own personalities_.
4- Finding the balance in _parenting_ pits and peaks.
5- The pits and pits in our _work lives._
6- The pits and peaks in our _human condition_.
7- Finding the "elder" balance between the pits/peaks of _old age,_

8- The Bible's <u>spiritual view</u> of the balancing virtues between pits & peaks.
9- <u>Conclusion</u>s regarding the recurrent themes and <u>patterns</u> in both the problems of pits/peaks and the resolution of resilience.

As a generality in the big picture map, our practice of heroic virtues would give us a resilience to overcome the despair of the pits as well as freedom from the addictions of the peaks. This practice of resilience would be the first component of our quest for "happiness" to help us bounce back from despair without taking on any fake cures which would bring the bondage rather than the freedom found in the true peaks. Given the reoccurrence of peaks and pits, what undermines our search for sustained stability?

Going by emotional reactivity to events is one source of instability. Stability comes from clearly discerned values followed by commitments and habits adjustable for different seasons of life. Stability comes from maturity not immaturity, being functional, not dysfunctional, rational, not irrational. Through responsibility and discipline, our character grows in its ability to discern and navigate between the ups and downs within ourselves as well as outside in our social and economic systems. Our character allows us to suffer loss or grief without running to the false comforts which distract us from needed lessons in the pits of life. Our characters grow from our integrity rather than escaping pain through the illusory relief of drugs or alcohol without virtue or insight. Only in the practice of **heroic virtues** throughout our lifespan crises do we find a path which combines dynamic **resilience with balanced stability** which promotes growth during both the ups (peaks) and downs (pits) of our lifespan changes.

If we were to tell the story of our lifespan, we would not begin with ourselves as semi-conscious babies but with the challenges of our parents "<u>falling</u> in love" and needing to learn how to "<u>stand</u> in love" through their pits and peaks. Only through our parents would we learn how we came into the world as babies and were guided through a loving dependency to grow into stages of independence and identity so critical for teens. One day, we would be fully functional working adults, married and finally able to experience the beginning stages of life from <u>both sides</u> (both as parent and infant) with full consciousness .

8.2—Balanced Resilience in the Peaks and Pits of <u>Marriage</u>

In our happiness journey to **marriage**, the peak of "falling in love" can lead to the pit of "falling out of love" without the <u>discipline and commitment</u> of "standing in love"(Fromm). The sexual passion for the opposite sex is the body's search for an <u>immediate intimacy</u> following nature's inbuilt desire to create a family. Sexual connection without <u>true friendship</u> can lead to the pits of being bonded to a stranger through the making of a baby together. The traditional sad result was an immature forced marriage rather than the free bonding of friendship grown through open, honest conversation and the sharing a variety of activities <u>over time.</u> Out of a sustained friendship through the ups and downs of two different personalities gradually grows a free choice commitment, chosen not forced.

Marriage must become a mix between "comfort circle" and a training center and for children to progress through most of the **eight stages** until children are launched from home to independent career training centers away from home. Having "secure attachments early in life promotes success both in peer relationships and in academic competence. A middle path parenting style combines both firm discipline with warm communication.

Parents must find a balance between childcare and fostering their own careers. This middle path becomes a lived example for the children to follow both as to co-parenting and two careers. Parents hope that their grown children find **career paths** which can satisfy both the **extrinsic and intrinsic** needs of the work realm. Workers need to make an adequate income but they also need to see their talents used and grown with the support of functional and ethical organizations.

Peaks and pits are built into our **human condition** which makes our journey a mix of wisdom and foolishness. The middle path requires humility to admit our mistakes and a mindful discipline to learn from our mistakes to avoid repeating the same lessons. Our human condition is also a mix of joyful and sad events especially as we face "old age, sickness and death". A middle path of celebrating joys and grieving losses all life long prepares us for "successful aging" within faith "comfort circles".

Stability in marriage is rooted in acceptance of both the peaks and pits which will come in any intimate relationship between two imperfect people. Compared to the single state, marriage can either **double your joys or double your sorrows.** Marriage can make your happiness wider, deeper and longer lasting. When it comes to our need for support through the hard times, marriage has the potential to **double our support** during the hard times if we have empathy and compassion for each other. Joy and support are the peak sides of marriage. We know that all things in life also have pit sides which are the reverse of the ideal.

In the course of normal life with normal partners, marriage can also **double our sorrows** as we experience not just our own troubles but that of our spouse. With double the trouble, our **burdens** are thereby **doubled** so you carry not just your own suffering and problems but that of your spouse. Single people may run away from such doubling of hardships but they would also be running away from **the doubling of support and joy.** The math still works out in favor of marriage since the doubling of burdens and sorrows are cut in half by the doubled support and joy both of which bring the couple closer to each other. When these struggles are shared with a common shared faith, another level of support and resilience is found.

With all the mix, research still shows that a "good fit marriage" is still one of the pillars of happiness despite its challenges since partners of long term marriages are happier than those who never married or divorced. These are the "vitalized, harmonious" marriages with adequate conflict resolution and communication satisfaction whose major values are shared. Nevertheless, at any given time, a couple may have to suffer through a prolonged pit where love seems far away and critical differences all around. During these pit times, it pays to remember, as has been said, that "angels can fly because they take themselves lightly."

Many singles parallel the role of parenting in their work as teachers, mentors and spiritual leaders. Some are religiously committed celibates who serve lay people and are integral parts of their own communities. As Mia, our young grand daughter said to our priest on Father's Day: "My dad is just a father to us but you are a father to everyone here!" Our book celebrates the call to joyful service and rich community both within and beyond our natural families.

8.3—Balanced Resilience in Personality Peaks and Pits

One perspective on personality differences is the "Enneagram" (nine types) which shows that all the nine personality types have some mix of strengths (peaks) and weaknesses (pits) **within themselves***. The Perfectionist and the Helper types may seem exceptional in virtues until we see how communication, conflict resolution, spiritual values, personality traits differences can lead to a devitalized and conflicted union rather than vitalized and harmonious.*

Different personality types must also find middle paths when partners differ in their needs for control and connection. The **Enneagram** shows contrasts both in people's needs for control and connection. Three of the nine types are high in their happiness needs for order and control. These three are Perfectionist (#1), the Achiever (#3), and the Asserter (#8) (see Kuby ch. 6). Three other types value connection more than control. These are the Helper (#2), the Peacemaker (#9), with a third, the Loyal Skeptic (#6) valuing <u>both</u> connection and control. For our purposes, we will only consider the paradoxical mix of the ups/downs typical of the Perfectionist and the Helper.

What can possibly be the problem for the **Perfectionist** (#1) who is "ethical, reliable, productive, wise, idealistic, fair, honest and disciplined" (Baron in Kuby, p 73)? Any employer would hire such a person of this character type in a minute. But hold on, there is actually a downside to this personality that they themselves (and their partners) feel. Perfectionists a can also be "judgmental, inflexible, dogmatic, can be obsessive-compulsive, tend to be critical of others, overly serious, controlling, anxious and jealous"(ibid.). Until the Perfectionist is aware of what they do not like about their personality, no movement toward a middle ground for a marriage would be possible. What do Perfectionists want to change.

Perfectionists like their **self-discipline** which allows them to achieve **excellence** but they do not like being disappointed with themselves for not meeting their own high standards and they rarely feel appreciated by others for trying to be the best employee, wife, mom that they can be.

One perfectionist author (B. Brown) found the peaks of perfectionism "self-destructive and addictive" and the pits of feeling alone, judged and fearful so painful that she saw imperfection as a help in finding her healing middle path of "wholeheartedness". (Brown in Kuby, p. 94). The heroic virtues she discovered for her happiness-recovery were the three c's of **courage, compassion and connection** to recover the wholeness of her true self (weaknesses and strengths) by letting go of blame, shame, and the rejection others have of her vulnerable imperfections. Brown came to see her **imperfection as a gift** to bring **forgiveness and acceptance** of her humanity which she now saw as a "blessing rather than a curse".

Can you imagine selling your Perfectionist partner on the "gift and blessing of imperfection"? Sounds like a job for God whose perfection and forgiveness make a good middle path as an "inside job". We are seeing our list of moderating virtues growing as we put together dance steps of self-discipline and courage as steps forward toward the happiness goal of excellence. The virtues of compassion, forgiveness, acceptance, compassion and connection seem to be steps in reverse of letting go to let God be God rather than the compulsion to play God. The "peak" of perfectionist happiness can be seen as a mix with addictive traps which need the reverse virtues of balance and freedom to move froward on the middle path to maturity.

The Helper/pleaser (#2) shows the love of connection by being "warm, caring, generous, sensitive, as well as enthusiastic and fun-loving." With these positive virtues for the desired happiness of connection, why would the Helper/pleaser want to change these positive qualities? Where would problems arise in a marriage to a controller type who might be attracted to the connector type to avoid conflicts over power issues.

Once a Helper type comes to therapy they will discover some downsides to their personality type. The helper is poor at setting limits and boundaries. They have a hard time saying "no" or confronting people. As a result the Helper suffers from low self-esteem and feels drained from overdoing for others. (Ibid., p.76). Helpers want to avoid being selfish so they do for others, put their own needs aside and then feel disappointed and resentful when their caregiving is not appreciated or reciprocated.

Coming into individual therapy, both the controller and the connector would be encouraged to use their strengths of their personality type to balance off their weaknesses. As we look at the strengths of each of these two types, it takes insight and humility to find their weaknesses so that they would tend to problems in their marriage with their partners who lack their strengths.

Up to this point, the flaws of Helpers seem to be in the normal range but without finding virtues toward a middle path, they can be on a slippery path into becoming annoying. Helpers tend to be "indirect and can become" manipulative, overly accommodating with their need to help others to the extreme of "codependency" where they encourage dependency rather than supporting independent assertiveness. The middle path of a balanced marriage requires both connection and confrontation to resolve conflicts. The personality conflicts between controller and connector require a "secure connection" to a God whose perfection is higher than the Perfectionist and whose love is deeper than the Helper. Both types need to come before a God who see all, forgives all, and blesses all with virtue to discover the middle paths away from the addictions of either perfectionism or codependency. Marriage naturally leads to another source of happiness as well as challenge with the birth of the first child.

8.4—Balanced Resilience in the Peaks and Pits of <u>Parenting</u> Children

The arrival of the first baby is a joyous celebration but also a new initiation through the challenges created by a vulnerable person needing 24/7 care and provision for every need. Betty Carter describes the early months with a newborn as a "shock" with "sleep deprivation, shredded schedules, endless chores" the need for "ceaseless vigilance" and parental fears of incompetence with this threat of chaos to overwhelm them. (Carter, p. 249) During this period, the ritual vows of marriage "for better and for worse" take on real meaning.

This latest initiation makes the heroic paradoxes of marriage real: marriage will double both your joys and sorrows, both your support and burdens, alternately stretch you into greater maturity and bring the stable comfort of intimate home life. Did we anticipate all this as we were preoccupied planning the perfect wedding and worrying how the two sets of in-laws would get along? We thought that we booked for the happiness train but ended up on the hero express.

You don't want your child to be spoiled as the "only child" so parents feel the need to have a second child which brings on sibling rivalry in the contest of superiority vs inferiority. The first born has to give up his/her throne as the center of family attention and feels inferior compared to all the fuss given the "latest and greatest". The project of the first born is to regain his first place by showing the younger one how superior he is in smarts and strength. Freud and Adler acted out their birth place differences with Freud being a controller (my way or the highway) until Adler finally left him to find his own theory of birth order. Adler as a middle child thought that this was the most objective place to not be caught up with either extreme. We see that the theme of power competition among children arises early if there are two children but it will have already happened in the child's preference of one parent over the other and in the "terrible (and wonderful) two's" assertion of their autonomy.

The teen years of rebellion and hormone-driven emotions will test the stability of the elementary school years as the teens seek more freedom and more separation from parents to find their own identities influenced by peers and the pop culture. The quest for identity is benchmark of major changes beginning with a crisis and ending with a resolution. The teen begins an exit from childhood into stages of adulthood around identity but the beginning of school outside the home began a long period of training into competence relative to peers. The superiority vs inferiority of sib rivalry takes a larger stage at school hopefully with balances. Some students are excellent in science and math whereas others may do best in the arts, languages and social sciences or excel in some sport. The stable love and support of parents are needed to offset feelings of inferiority coming from peer competition at school. The heroic virtue of true humility is seeing both your weaknesses and strengths and finding ways for your strengths to offset weaknesses.

The "empty nest" is both a release and a challenge. Parents are released from the ongoing demands of teenagers but now face the challenge of finding out who they are separate from their parenting roles. New demands for greater intimacy may cause more conflicts but there is more uninterrupted time for the couple to improve their skills in communication and conflict resolution. Another crisis means another initiation into heroic virtues of growth and maturity.

Midlife for parents is now late life for their parents (the grandparents of their children on both sides). Parents want to support "successful aging" and aging in place for their parents as they face the limitations or health issues of old age. The two gears of holding on and letting go need to be used since the aging parents do not want the roles reversed in a way that undermines their freedom of choice without respect for their many years of experience. At the end, the grandparents will have their final transition in the context of loving family as they find their release from their bodies into a new spiritual world. This is a foreshadowing of what the parents will go through as they become grandparents, elderly and then leave this human family.

The underlying eight stages of Erikson's lifespan theory are well-supported with minor modifications. When we meet the challenges of each stage, we have strengths in love and power in these eight stage options but the unhappiness outcomes are stark. Lacking parental consistency (or good substitutes) will we end up struggling with mistrust, doubt, guilt, inferiority, a confused, conflicted identity, isolated from failure to give to the next generation, and finally despair at the end of our lives?

When infants begin life with secure attachment with continued family support, the outcome is more likely to have the positive outcomes: to establish **trust, autonomy, initiative, competence at work, an integrated identity, intimacy in marriage which generates new life, and acceptance of one's life as a whole with its peaks and pits.** These are the results of the habitual practice of middle path virtues of parents, peers **and mentors. Those who have had gaps in their own childhoods may be inspired to fill these gaps for their children following their own personal work in therapy and/ or spiritual healing.**

The lifespan data lead us to the possibilities of a lifelong marriage and a lifelong career with positive connections to the next generations of adult children and their children even though 50% of marriages end in divorce. Experiencing the loss of an intimate spouse through divorce or death can be life shattering leaving the one left behind grief-stricken and lonely. The evidence from marriage counseling has confirmed the importance that Erikson has given to achieving secure attachment as a child for its role in the later dynamics of marriage as we have seen with the marital mismatches of the "Vacillator" (too much fighting) and the "Avoider" "(too much "flighting" in order to avoid fighting}. Work is required in marriage for good conflict resolution and real communication and work is required outside the home for adequate income.

Work is needed to support a family but using one's talents in a career is also a source of happiness with the development of the heroic virtues of competence and discipline.

8.5 —Balanced Resilience in the Pits and Peaks of <u>Work</u>

"Love and work are the cornerstones of our happiness according to Freud and the research supports the roles of both a stable marriage and stable long term career. Needing a single focus, our book has chosen the work within marriage and parenting with a secondary concern for careers outside the home as key essentials for supporting and raising children for eighteen years at home and college. With the heavy college debt and unreal expense of real estate, support may be needed until parents pay for the cost of a wedding and help with grand children when adult children are close to 30. Parents must find fulfillment from their work to buffer the ups and downs of long-term parenting as part of their heroic pursuit of happiness.

Studs Terkel tells us that "jobs are too small for our spirits" and that we need a calling that gives us purpose and meaning in our lives to "manifest our hidden talents for the benefit of our human community" so that we find "dignity and self esteem". (Kuby, ch. 7.4, p.90) We spend half of our lives working as one source of fulfillment but Terkel found a recurrent message of "discontent" (unhappiness) from a lack of good-fit job which allows the worker to use his talents to benefit society with the proper pay. Terkel heard these complaints: "I'm a machine" (spot welder), "I'm caged (bank teller), "I'm a robot" (accountant). (Kuby, p.90)

Terkel saw "the automated pace" of our work as the heart of the problem as name, face and emotions are made invisible. There is a desire to be remembered for our unique, creative style of work like the arthritic waitress who does her work like a ballerina. The longing for dignity at work gives rise to titles like "building engineer" (janitor), "account executive (salesman), "sanitary Waste Manager" (garbage man). The industrial revolution "dehumanized" work wherein each factory worker makes only one part of the whole with none of the satisfaction of the craftsman who takes satisfaction in creating the whole from start to finish. Workers need to see that their work is essential for the greater good of society more than just meeting their survival needs. Work is meant to meet certain "intrinsic" needs of our humanity.

What are some of the intrinsic goals achieved by a stable, long lasting career? American adults derive much of their identity, self-concept, life satisfaction, and life meaning through their work" . Major intrinsic goals of work include the self-actualization goals of growth, creativity, and autonomy. Maslow saw a hierarchy of needs beyond survival which including a sense of life's purpose and meaning, finding truth and the experience transcendence found in "peak experiences" which are times of heightened happiness wherein we rise above worldly problems to have new insights, perspective and inspiration.

Individuals find meaning in their work when they feel that they are growing professionally and moving forward into avenues with new skills to improve themselves guided by a code of ethics, responsibility, and morality.

A sense of connectedness is also important at work when employees have a spirit of collaboration with co-workers with a sense of community and feel that they are contributing to something bigger than themselves.

By contrast, dysfunctional organizations have debilitating consequences to self-esteem and self-concept. Feelings of self-doubt about one's competence, direction in life, and future possibilities are common. The same is true for those laid off unemployed individuals in general but with men being more affected than women. Marriage and social support help the mental health of unemployed women but less so for men whose identities are traditionally defined as family breadwinners. Today roles have changed in some families where the wife is working outside the home while the husband is fulfilling the duties of the home.

8.6—Resilience in the Pits and Peaks of Our "Human Condition"

Charles Davis describes the imperfections and limited achievements due to our "human condition".

"Life is...an untidy mess of unfinished business, broken achievements, personal failures, half successes, short-lived triumphs, belated insights,] noble desires and shameful deeds...(so that) life remains an incomplete and unsavory jumble...an untidy mess." (cited in Heroism, Kuby, pp 95,104)

Davis goes on to admit that we have "momentary flashes of joy" and "moments of breathtaking perfection" which become "vehicles carrying us to the transcendent" but only if we do not try to possess them. (ibid, 95-6). These flashes of joy are meant to inspire us to the work of heroism which leads us to "love, meaning, hope, transcendence, connectedness and compassion, true values and creativity" according to Cory who describes the milieu in which the best versions of ourselves are fostered. (Ibid. p. 96).

As seen in the section on work, despite our human condition, we have a desire to be more than we are, to be aspired by **excellence** wherever we see it in the Super Bowl winners in sports, the surpassing technology of our cyber revolution, our secular and religious timeless heroes. Our foolishness.wisdom ratio in everyday life made the average person ordinary, but each one of us has special talents and passions that make us extraordinary. For example, neither of my parents graduated from high school, but my passion for religious answers pressed me on to get an Mdiv and PhD from excellent schools giving witness to the miracle of the right fit connections of interest and talents. On the other hand, I am below ordinary in generating a high income, doing home repairs, mastering math or being an all around athlete. The over and under achievements put me in the middle path mix with my own peaks and pits. The stable, steady middle path requires an ongoing set of virtues from our higher selves and resistance against the worst vices of our lower selves. The middle path is "fighting the good fight" and "running the good race" to become the best stewards we can be with our God-given gifts to become the best versions of ourselves throughout our long distance run.

Mother Theresa sees all the disappointments of our "Human Condition" and urges us to make heroic decisions anyhow.

> "People are often unreasonable, irrational, and self-centered. FORGIVE THEM ANYWAY. (with God's grace)... Give the best you have and it will never be enough. Give your Best Anyway. In the final analysis, IT IS BETWEEN YOU AND GOD. It was never between you and them anyway."

For these non-religious seculars in crises, there is a starting point with the "Serenity Prayer" which guides twelve step support groups to find the wise middle path between courageous battles for change and the serenity of a peaceful acceptance. "God, grant me the Serenity To accept the things I cannot change... Courage to change the things I can, And Wisdom to know the difference...accepting hardship as the pathway to peace" which is only possible by trusting in God "to make all things right if I surrender to His will." Take this imperfect world as it is (not as I would have it) and expect to be "reasonably happy in this life" knowing that we will be "supremely happy with God in the next."

*For some, dealing with the limitations and pain of old age is harder than facing death itself. Traditional societies around the world have a status called "**elders**" for those who have already raised a family and retired from their careers who need a role which gives new meaning and purpose to their lives.*

8.7—Balanced Resilience in the Pits and Peaks of our "Elder" Stage

As we approach old age, we can choose the *role of an "Elder" as a way of balanced resilience to reconcile the peaks and pits of our last stage of life. We also have a spectrum of other choices as we become less involved with parenting and our careers as grandparents and retired seniors. How do we find both balance and resilience outside of our normal roles as parents and full-time employed workers? The following are some reflections from a variety of sources reflecting on what is possible for the elderly.*

Elders can *choose to live life as fully as possible by* **compensating** *experience and wisdom for speed and stamina. Elders can choose* **optimism** *over pessimism to bounce back with effective coping of daily problems.*

Elders can set clear goals in life to not give up what they see as their God-given calling in life by embracing necessary losses to face to exceed their own limitations. Elders can choose to follow their call in life beyond work duties seeking to develop a deeper spiritual that shows the meaning and purpose of this stage of life. Elders may want to live more connected to the sacred to find peace and compassion.

Elders may choose to celebrate pruning and downsizing of those things no longer essential to their minds and hearts to help seek what are the true essentials in this stage of life.

Elders can seek to integrate the lessons of earlier stages to help serve others in need through prayer-led actions and embrace the lessons of humility in the aging process to "fall upward" where grace is found. (These resolves are gleaned from authors on the spirituality of aging including R. Rohr's **Falling Upward,** Singh's **The Grace of Aging**).

The elder seeks the balanced resilience between denial of aging and being overcome by aging by *accessing strengths from experience to compensate for weakness from aging. We need heroes like those who have overcome cancer and traumas to enlighten and inspire us from their first hand experiences of resilience against the odds.*

D.F. Pollets was "knocked off his feet" when he suddenly received a diagnosis of stage iii "colorectal CANCER when he was so sure that he was healthy and fit. ("Pollets, P-T, Growth. 6/20). To survive both cancer and Post Traumatic Stress (PTS), Pollets had to allow his suffering to so "plow up the surface of his life" to uncover depths of greater strength that would "rebuild the infrastructure of his life" which he calls "PTG" or Post- Trauma Growth (Ibid. p. 7). Survival from late stage cancer would require a "hybrid mix" of active work through changes as well as passive surrender to the nine month impact of chemotherapy infusions and radiation in order for the patient to "bounce forward and thrive". (Ibid. p.7) Spirituality and social support were two sources of "acceptance coping" for the "recognizing the universality of a particular suffering" through a network of intimate personal relationships (Ibid. 7) Pollets began with a "profound anxiety", was very sick with a vital function of 5% efficiency and had to fight "future catastrophic thinking". With the "secure attachment" of his wife, therapist and close friends, Pollets could openly express his "fears, worries and hopes" which reduced his stress and made him feel loved and not alone. Through mindfulness, meditation and the power of expressing gratitude he felt empowered to focus on the positive here and now rather than worries of the future or feeling powerless over his terminal illness and how to find meaning and purpose as he experienced the finite nature of out earthly life. Pollets ends by agreeing with the higher power "grace" described by Ram Das.

"**Fierce grace is a gift,** an inexplicable and **surprising capacity to** cope with, and **grow through, a difficult life circumstance**... Somehow some deeper, wiser part of us does move through (our crisis). We find that something out there and "in here' that is bigger than me supports me in very surprising ways." (Ibid. 9)

8.8—The Balanced Resilience of the Bible through Pits and Peaks

The Bible reveals both the wrong and the right ways to deal with our core sin of pride. Satan sought the peak and found himself in the pits as seen in Isaiah 14:12.

> "How you are fallen from heaven, O Lucifer, son of the morning! For you have said in your heart: 'I will ascend into heaven, I will exalt my throne above the stars of God; I will be like the Most High.'
>
> Yet you shall be brought down to Sheol, To the lowest depths of the Pit."

Our pride leads us to make God small so that we can make ourselves bigger and better to take over and play god. That reversal was already tried once and it didn't work out so well for Lucifer. Unfortunately, Lucifer's rebellion didn't work out so well for us humans either as described later in Rev. 12:-9.

The impact of our original sin happened before Eden with Satan's prideful warfare against God. Sadly humans followed Satan in rebellion rather than submitting in obedience to God's law. Correction to man's deep pride is found in Paul's Philippians 2:5-8.

> "Let this mind be in you which was also in Christ Jesus: Who, existing in the form of God, did not consider equality with God something to be grasped, but emptied Himself, taking the form of a servant, being made in human likeness. And being found in appearance as a man, He humbled Himself and became obedient to death—even death on a cross".

Our correction to the false peak of pride is through the humility of the Cross of Christ who integrates the extremes of spiritual pits and peaks.

"In him all the fullness of God was pleased to dwell, and through Him **to reconcile to himself all things,** whether on earth or in heaven, making peace **by the blood of his cross."**

Christ's resurrection from the dead reconciled the opposites of life and death by "killing" death and freeing Life from death forever more at the spiritual level. Our human condition is between **"the already"** (Christ's victory over death) and **"the not yet"** (our victory) which requires the middle path of faith in God's promises shown by past awesome deeds. The Middle path over the happiness gap of our human condition is through the person of Jesus Christ who reconciles all opposites through the power of his death and resurrection. Jesus is our hero par excellence who is the Way through all the conflicts, divisions, polarities. Our first stumbling block to find a balanced middle path in Christ is paradox. Jesus had had power and prestige but would be condemned to the shameful death of a blasphemer with a public execution on a cross. The resurrection which followed was enough to kill one man's "faith in Atheism" as told by Leo Strobel. **After his death, Jesus appeared** to groups of people on three different occasions which included **five hundred people** seeing him all at the same time as **confirmed by eight different ancient sources** of the time. Both Christ's death and resurrection were too overwhelming. Strobel concluded that **it would "take more faith to sustain his atheism" than to believe the Gospel.**

Christ lived out paradox particularly at the time of His death on the cross when he cried out "My God, my God, why have you forsaken me?" *(Ps. 22:1,6) As Jesus was dying, He quoted Psalm 22's first words of abandonment with the completion of faith hanging as those witnessing knew the acclamation of faith of this Psalm. When an unrighteous thief hanging on the cross beside Him spoke in faith, with confidence Jesus could say* **"this day you will be with me in paradise**. *What consolation for all of us imperfect people as we face our own deaths. In this way, Christ was able to express both the suffering of our humanity and the transcendence of faith that came from His unity to the Father.*

Many living people (eight million NDE documented cases) have already proved that Jesus' resurrection was the first fruit of our passing from the painful cross of death into a blissful rebirth outside our physical bodies. (Kuby, p. 28) When outside their bodies, the newly dead person experiences a personal "Being of Light" who is both "an astonishing, unconditional love" as well as "power itself" who is completely accepting and understanding but asks the question "How much have you loved with your life" (as a whole to make your life worthwhile)?? And this was a question "that hung in the dazzling air. (Ibid. 31) Those with near death experiences (NDE) cover a spectrum range of faiths through no-faith but the most common identification of the "Being of Light" is Jesus. Whatever their faith (or no faith), people report "an irresistible magnetic attraction" with whom they communicate beyond words and are perfectly understood with personal love, warmth and humor. Faith seems to be a lesser problem for those outside their bodies except for those programmed to reject the light to choose darkness and evil leading to a form of spiritual death.

8.9—Balanced Resilience through Pits and Peaks Conclusions

Let us examine how balanced resilience varies in different contexts as to its ability to integrate or reconcile the opposites of peaks and pits. How do the heroic virtues bring forth character and the better self? What is the balance of wisdom versus foolishness in mix of our human condition? What is the pattern of spiritual "fingerprints" of an unseen metaphysical reality which address the ultimate struggles of life against death, truth over illusions, good against evil and a transcendent meaning to life rather than the repeated tragedy of the Titanic's Big Goodbye?

We began with the idea of "falling in love" like the idealized passions of two lovers wherein "momentary flashes of joy" became vehicles which carry us to the transcendence of beauty, breathtaking perfection and intimate love against the backdrop of the "untidy mess" of our human condition.

The broken-hearted apostles of Jesus tried to make sense of an apparent tragic murder of their Messiah. Jesus walked with them, unrecognized in his resurrected body, and gave them the Big Picture overview from Scripture that Jesus had **already** come as a **suffering servant** but would **not yet** come as their expected Messiah who would bring justice and freedom to God's chosen people. Despite this disappointment, Peter made the point "where else do we go to find someone who forgives sin and heals diseases? Finally Jesus showed that he also had the power to "kill death" through the demonstration of His resurrection. Clearly, He is "the Way, the Truth and the Life" but following Him would lead Peter to his own cross like the other apostles (except for John). To truly follow Jesus, we must love Him more than our own lives, and only in losing our lives will we find true life. This impossible challenge was another paradox like those of the Beatitudes which show that the last will be first and our mourning will be blessed. We are challenged to hold two opposing ideas at once. The opposites of death and life, loss and gain, sin and merciful forgivers are all reconciled in the God-man Jesus Christ who dies for us and and is fully risen to eternal life as witnessed by his disciples never to be subject to death again. How can we understand these paradoxes and have the courage to go against our human nature to put Jesus above our own survival? We have been given a source of both wisdom beyond our understanding and courage through the presence of the Holy Spirit beyond us and within us as we are Born again as new creations in Christ but our journey continues to be a paradox until **the not yet** becomes **the already.** We can't think it out logically we can only live it out.

Our life's journey is under this big screen larger than life of classic lovers, martyrs, heroes, but we live our ordinary lives with our "broken achievements...half successes and short-lived triumphs" living our scaled down versions of heroic challenges. The balanced resilience we find as we live out the crises of our lifespan inspired and sustained by the resilience of Christ's victory over both physical death and spiritual death in the cosmic battle of God's goodness against diabolical evil.

We have a choice to be deformed by the pits of trouble or we can be informed by its lessons to seek those virtues which will bring reform to our lives and characters to better serve the greater good. During the hard times, we don't need faith to be hurt by evil but we need a resilient faith to realize God's light when we are lost in darkness. Where sin abounds, grace abounds more. Is there a single source and focus which allows us to grow consistently through both the peaks and pits of life? Do we have a mentor and companion for all the seasons of our life?

The New Testament reveals from first hand witnesses that Jesus is our source of reconciliation and resilience for every conflict, battle, division, divorce, war, death. According to the New Testament, Jesus does not just show us the way to overcome the pits of sin and death, He Is the <u>WAY</u> (the I AM) who leads us to <u>Truth</u> and to the fullness of Life. How can we understand that Christ is present with us in our humanity? Paul gives us an integral metaphor when he tells us that "we have this treasure in earthen *vessels, that the excellency of the power may be revealed.* Through this "excellency" of Christ's power, Paul was able to bear persecution and trials to carry the gospel over sea and land, in the midst of danger and opposition. Through the living "treasure" of Christ's light within him, Paul was able to transcend the limitations of being a mere earthen vessel to become be an instrument of conversion to share the treasure entrusted to the faithfulness of the one small nation of Israel now to be given to all of mankind as the sacred law of His "Chosen People' was now able by grace to be written in the hearts of all people over all the earth for all times.

CHAPTER NINE

BALANCED RESILIENCE THROUGH LIFE'S PEAKS AND PITS: THE POWER AND LOVE OF HEROIC MENTORS FOR THE KUBY FAMILY

9.1—Finding the Resilient Self through Life's Pits and Peaks

Our **true self** is found as we **bounce back** from losses in life **inspired and guided by mentors** who help us bring victories out of near defeats.

We learn the virtues of resilience as children. When he was six my nephew, Eric played basketball with the key elements of heroism. The game was hard-fought with endurance and skill and now the final second would make the difference between victory or defeat. Eric had faith in himself and the courage to make that final shot. When he made it and pulled out a last second victory in his imagination he heard all the fans loudly, joyfully celebrating his heroic victory.

Eric had difficulties in reading and, as his uncle with experience in this area, I became his tutor. As a reward for hard work in reading exercises, Eric would go to his backyard to "shoot hoops" with a skill that he then lacked in reading. Success in basketball became of symbol of resilience in academic tests of progress. Eric could make a variety of shots inspired his professional heroes and though his imagination visualized success on the big stage with the appropriate fanfare and celebration.

By the time he was a senior in high school, Eric would make those last minute shots for victories with real fans and celebrations thanks to skill and hours of practice. The confidence and self-esteem from sports transferred over to academics and Eric would graduate high school, college and grad school to become a professional mastering the ups and downs of the stock market to bring economic resilience.

Later in life, I would have two daughters who would love the stories of "Sheroes" who would bring resilience to allow good to defeat evil. Heroic stories were not interesting unless there was a real battle which took victory out a near or seeming defeat against the odds from Cinderella to the Little Mermaid or Lion King. Childhood entertainment was "marinated" in the heroic resilience which would transfer to the normal challenges of life inspired by mentors. One daughter, Beth, would join her friends successfully in every kind of sport and would become a mom of my two grandchildren. The other daughter, Rebekah, chose to pursue her version of creative lifestyle outside the box connecting with innovative job mentors to learn landscaping skills which would serve communities in diverse areas with a committed partner but without children.

Thus we see two different visions of dedicated heroic lifestyles within the same family.

Even as children as we follow our favorite teams, we find that any given season will have ups and downs like the peaks and pits we experience in our everyday lives. Sports provide the symbolism for our quest for resilience but our everyday life requires developing the virtues needed to overcome the negativity of the pits and the false hopes of the peaks. Sports requires the sustained discipline to master essential skills and the courage to take on superior opponents. We may hate those opponents who overcome us too often but we don't really believe that superior teams are evil.

From fairy tales to opera and Shakespeare, creative literature exposes us to the battle of good against evil. Our religious traditions take us behind what is seen to explain how humans can become evil through an unseen spirit of evil which exploits our human mix of good and evil. In today's world, we see evil taking a tangible form as Putin bombs children and women civilians in schools and hospitals. Hitler was another extreme example of evil taking a human form.

For most of our lives, we battle against some spectrum of good versus in evil in our political and economic struggles which require heroic virtues for resilience.

Jesus appears in the Gospels as a classic hero. Jesus delivers the possessed from demons, brings Lazarus back from death, confronts the injustices by the Romans and the Pharisees, and appears as the new Moses who will set God's Chosen people free. The followers of Jesus wanted to crown Him as King like King David and Solomon to restore the lost "Golden Age" of righteous power. After Jesus was put to death, his disciples were confused and disappointed that He was not the awaited Messiah that He appeared to be.

After His resurrection, Jesus would remind His flock that He was first to be the "Suffering Servant" as prophesied in Isaiah in order to save His people from sin.

God's kingdom would come from within through the power of Christ's death and the release of the Holy Spirit. We would be changed from within not by external laws and kings but by laws written within our hearts and God's inner kingdom.

One day God's kingdom would be established upon the whole earth among all the people but through a sacred reversal. The first will be last and the last first. The poor in spirit will be blessed and mourners will be comforted with hope. We are forgiven as we forgive, and receive love as we give it, even to the least and the undeserving. Jesus would be resurrected from the dead and we would all follow Christ's lead through resilience over different forms of death through the ups and downs of our daily lives. Every example of resilience in our lives would feed the longing of our souls for God's tangible presence in our life.

If evil could become a tangible reality, why not the presence of God who rescues us from evil through the power of good over evil, and life over death?

To see this resilience in our personal lives, we must each reflect upon the challenges and victories in our personal lives for which the story of the Kuby extended family provides a small but tangible example. We are all challenged to put together what is **"already"** (the victory of Christ's death) with what is **"not yet"** (our daily victories over evil within our lives).

Our story examines our resilience as a family through our lives' peaks and pits over our lifespans. Following an overview of our topic (9.1), resilience is examined in ten settings from our grandparents' roots in Czechoslovakia (9.2) to the sibs becoming grandparents. All six sibs began their young lives in the Parmadale orphanage for 4-5 years (9.3) until they were united as a family in Cleveland's Wade Park area (9.4) and then exiled to live with relatives in Johnstown (9.5) where the author found his resilience over a nine year period with shorter stays for the older sibs. Three of the brothers (9.6) had to find their resilience in the military during wartime and moving into marriage after two or three years and finding their careers. Now alone, David, was helped by mentors to find his resilience out of pit situations (9.7) until he found a spiritual resilience in his faith and work (9.8) leading to his marriage and family, the death of his wife, Jan, and a resilience into a new life with Gail (9.9). The last section (9.10) reflects on the sunsets of his sibs in recent years and the new search for resilience during the inevitable losses of family in our late years. Let us begin our lifespan journey through time over four score years seeing how resilience lifts us up out from life's hardships and challenges into a deeper life.

9.2—Roots and Resilience in Extended Family Beginnings

The story of our family has its roots in Eastern Europe before the disasters of two world world wars and the takeover of communism in Czechoslovakia. Our grandparents came seeking political freedom and work found in Western Pennsylvania where the Bethlehem Steel Mills provided hard manual labor for those lacking English or higher education. Their Catholic faith would provide a Slovak speaking church and community where they could raise a large family and finally find their rest in a Catholic Slovak cemetery. Our father, Paul, found that Slovaks got worse job duties with lower pay and so he and his brothers legally changed their names from the Slovak, "Kubofcik" to the Austrian/German version of "Kuby". Lest our roots be discovered, we were forbidden to speak Slovak in our home which made us feel ashamed of our identity. Decades later my brothers discovered the high culture and intelligence of the city of Prague, capital of the unified country.

As we began to have family reunions later in life, our eldest brother Tom did research to show us the resilience of our grandparents, Jan and Maria Kubofcik. Jan Kubofcik (born December 1861) and Maria Sirocky (born December 1864) were both born in Dubrava, a small town in the central mountainous region of Slovakia in the eastern part of Czechoslovakia. The Slavic people came to this "Spis area" around 700 A.D., were subject to Feudal lords and the Ottoman empire Turks. Later the Austrian-Hungarian Empire would try to make Hungarian language and culture dominant in our cherished Slovak culture which inspired our grandfather to leave his known home in Eastern Europe for an unknown future in an unknown country. Jan Kubofcik arrived in the USA in December 1880 at the age of 24 with the virtues of courage, determination and discipline for his needed resilience.

Immigrants, even without English or education, knew that they could find employment with the Bethlehem Steel Mills in Johnstown. Jan would find work doing hard manual labor in the Steel Mills which he would do all this life. Two years after his arrival in Johnstown, Jan would marry Maria at his local Catholic (and Slovak) Church, the Immaculate Conception. In 5/1889, Maria lost four of her relatives in the Johnstown flood which killed 2,209 people requiring discernment and determined resilience to continue living in Johnstown. As bad as the flood was, by leaving Eastern Europe when they did, our family was spared the suffering of two world wars with Germany and the communist take-over by Russia. Their Catholic faith led and comforted our grandparents until they found their final resting in a cemetery that was both Catholic and Slovak after living long lives and leaving behind a large family for future generations.

Jan and Maria would have five daughters (Clara, Anna, Elizabeth, Mary and Verna) and four sons (John, Paul, George and Joe) with our father, Paul, being the 2nd oldest son but the 5th born in the family in 5/1889. World War I would involve Dad's first born brother, John, in years of trench warfare battling the Germans in France. John then worked as a fireman for the next 30 years and would host Dad's three youngest sons from ten months (Ray) to nine years (David). John lived his life in Johnstown unharmed by another flood that came in 1970.

Johnstown was a "city that flood waters couldn't kill" according to a local song celebrating the resilience of this city.

Our father, Paul, would join the army just after the war ended to be stationed in Honolulu, Hawaii where he worked as a carpenter and cook. After the war, at the age of 26, **Paul Kuby** married the 18 year old **MaryAnn Gabany** 6/24/1924 in a Catholic Church in Johnstown (St. Francis). (see ***Photo #1**). Their marriage certificate was written in Slovak, a language treasured by the extended families on both sides since they had come to America to preserve their cultural identity from Hungarian dominance.

Our mother, MaryAnn, was something of a "Cinderella" figure. Her real mother had died when MaryAnn was only two years old soon followed by the remarriage of her father giving her an unloving stepmother who pulled her out of early elementary school to work long hours on their farm, leaving MaryAnn with little education, and later leaving our father with a promise to never remarry.

Paul and MaryAnn had their first daughter, Rita, a year after their marriage in 7/1925 and then their first son. Tom, a year later in 12/1926, with the two of them receiving their first holy communion together when Tom was six and Rita seven. Tom recalls his love of the "magic of Christmas" with its "fragrance of pine, ornaments and gifts" as an abiding memory of his religious life before going into the Parmadale orphanage. (T. Kuby, "Journey for Life's Meaning", p.7)

Younger sister Jane would be born in June 1928, with a younger brother Don born in November 1929 (when the stock market crashed) at the beginning of the great depression waiting for Roosevelt to bring on the "New Deal". In 1934, grandfather Jan Kubofcik died at 73 to be buried in a Catholic Slovak cemetery to join his wife Maria who had died seven years earlier.

Our dad was supporting seven children as a manual laborer in Otis Steel while our mother was put into the hospital. Then it was that the three sons (Tom, Don and Ray) would be sent to the orphanage in Parmadale on the Westside of Cleveland while the two daughters, Rita and Jane, were sent to a girls' orphanage (St. Joseph's) in the inner city on the East side. Unlike the brothers, neither of the two sisters wrote anything about their experiences in their orphanage. Both the brothers and the sisters would be cared for by our Catholic supported orphanages for the next five years. Finally, Dennis joined the brothers in 1938 first in a "fondling home" and then the "baby cottage" where Ray had stayed from his 4th to his 6th years of age.

9.3—Resilience in the Orphanage for Brothers Ray and Tom

Just as our roots in Eastern Europe impacted us culturally, the family's five years in an orphanage at the time of my birth impacted our values and perspectives as a family.

This first photograph of **seven sibs (Photo #2)** was taken 6/9/40 on the grounds of the Parmadale orphanage by our unseen father with our mother wearing black in the middle of the assembled children. Ray comments on this photo as he introduces each of the seven sibs reflecting on the various reactions from surprised acceptance to shocked upset ((Ray's essay "Safe Haven, 3/2/2020). (*Note: Author's self references vary between "David" and "I/me").

Ray describes himself in the photo as "stiffly erect and **looking very grim"** - seemingly disappointed in yet another baby when sent off at age 4 (8.5 years old in this photo). Behind Ray is Rita, 14, touching Ray's left shoulder affectionately who remained Ray's closest ally in the family. Rita would enter the work world as a secretary as soon as she could in order to avoid the required housework and childcare for those staying at home. This work fell to her younger sister, Jane, who later as an adult became a loving mom.

Next in the photo and in age is Tom, 13, who is unsmiling with his head turned from the camera to hide a **large birthmark** on the left side of his face which had become a source of ridicule for bullies for which Tom compensated with achievements. As Ray indicates, "Tom was **artistic and athletic**. Tom played the coronet in the school's marching band and was immersed in the religious rituals" both as an altar boy and choir member. (Ibid. p.4) Ray notes that while he was very close to Rita he was never close to Tom for a "variety of reasons", nor did Tom and Rita get along very well.

Our mother appears, 35, is seen in the center of the photo dressed in black as she holds me as a 3 month old baby. Jane is on her left and she would soon become the **mother substitute** when the family returned to our Wade Park home during our mother's later illness and death.

Don, the charismatic, dramatic storyteller brother, is seen in front of Jane gently holding David's left foot with affection. From Ray's perspective, Don seemed to have been the smartest in the family but he would choose a "very **complicated life on the edge**" (which seemed foolish).

Ray goes on to describe both the peaks and pits of life in the Parma orphanage. In contrast to the hard times facing Paul and MaryAnn, Ray recalls "many fond experiences growing up in Parmadale" such as athletic activities and musical training. (Kuby, Safe Haven. p5) Ray recalls sled riding and ice skating in winter, swimming in summer, and competition with other schools in basketball, and having stories read by volunteer ladies. Ray was in school at the orphanage from Kindergarten to Fourth Grade but his most lasting memory was the nun's mantra: "order is Heaven's First Law, without discipline nothing is possible." (RK. Ibid. p.5) In conclusion, Ray saw the Parmadale as a "very desirable alternative to life in Cleveland during the depression (which put him)... in much better shape, physically and mentally than the boys in his 5th grade class when he returned to Cleveland." (ibid, p.6) So it was that Parmadale would be the first chapter in the story as our faith and family requiring resilience through the mix of peaks and pits. Ray choose to see more of the benefits of his five years in the orphanage but some renamed it "Parma Jail" due to the institutional discipline and limits on freedom.

The older brother Tom chose resilience over the hardships of the orphanage by seizing the opportunities provided for him to excel in sports and music. Tom played the trumpet in a 40 piece marching band, sang in the choir and had chances to hear operas and see ballet performances. Tom also excelled in basketball with his speed (nicknamed "Frisky"). Music and sports gave resilience in the emphasis on order over nurturing love. Nicknames gave a sense of kinship so Ray became "Buzz" and Don was "Chippy". Later Tom would call David "Pepe Le Moko" after seeing the film ***Algiers*** with Charles Boyer.

Discipline and order were the principles followed to keep order with 40 boys in each cottage. In keeping with the ideal of disciplined order, the routine at Parmadale for the brothers was to be awakened at 6 a.m in order to go to an early Mass to be followed by a small breakfast, school classes, music lessons and finally study in the evening. Each month, parents could visit and bring fruit which was subject to being shared with other orphans.

The youngest in the orphanage was our brother **Dennis** seen at six years old in the photo who provided us with a rare photo memory from Parmadale. **Father Gallagher** was a popular priest who would be re-assigned after years serving the orphanage, Dennis jumped up on the priest's lap looking sadly to be the subject of a photo titled "Best of Friends Must Part". (**Photo #3)**. This would be the first newspaper photos showing how Dennis could "seize the moment" to become newsworthy which he would later do selling Peanuts at a sports stadium and then in his life as a Unitarian minister dramatizing issues of social justice or protection of the ecology of our planet.

As we seek a balanced perspective, we see the generosity of the provision of the Catholic Church to support six children over a five year period.

My sibs reported a mix of neurotic/mean nuns mixed with kind, saintly ones which was the same mix I experienced in nine years of parochial school.

With the increased work from World War II, our father could bring us all home again as a united family but the transition from an orderly institution to the chaos of what would become a home without parents with our dad working two job shifts and our mom struggling with health issues. Large families were often a norm at this time without resulting in tragedy. Dad's younger brother, Joe had seven children without medical challenges.

9.4—Reunion and Resilience in Our Wade Park Home

At nine years old, Ray found his transition from the predictable order of the Orphanage to the "chaos" of life with seven children in Cleveland's inner city at 7009 Wade Park. Ray lacked "street smarts" and was intimidated by the lack of order in the public playgrounds where no one seemed to be "in charge". What should have been a happy reunion to home was made difficult by limited parental involvement. Our mom was ill with a complicated pregnancy with dad busy working overtime to support our family. Living on a tight budget made buying food for seven children difficult as was doing laundry without the labor saving devices which we enjoy now. During the 1940's, the laundry had to be done by hand using a scrub board followed by drying the clothes on a line outside despite the year-round unpredictable rains in the Cleveland area.

Ray recalls that his first real contact with Dennis was shortly after his seventh birthday because Dennis was separated from the other brothers Dennis was first put in a "fondling home" and then later transferred to the baby cottage on the Parmadale grounds. Therefore, the friendship between Ray and Dennis only began after the family resettled in their Wade Park home. (**Photo #4**) At first, Ray connected as a "typical big brother" until Ray became aware of Dennis' special qualities which he described as: Dennis' **"unflappable demeanor, persistence, ingenuity, kindness and good nature"** which made them lifelong good friends. (R. Kuby, 5/18/19)

Ray appreciated the liveliness which the teenage sibs brought into our Wade Park home: "Tom's drawings, Don's stories, the various friends of Rita and Jane" even though Dad had problems dealing with their dating. (ibid, p. 5). Ray and Dennis enjoyed getting on the street cars for 2 cents to see baseball games, movies and parks. Soon I would be added to this adventure club of two between the age of 4 to 5 even though I slowed them down. Dennis had made a promise to be my caretaker which he could only do with my inclusion in the outings.

Tom recalls that the Wade Park years (1941-45) were more liberating and joyous than the orphanage with new found friends and activities, and "feelings of triumph to be reunited as a family" but there was a downside when our dad pulled him out of school at 15 in order to work to help support the family. As the eldest male sib, Tom would have to drop out of school to work a full-time job and then hand over most of his paycheck to dad to help support the family following the tradition of our father's family. (TK, Journey, 5/96).

Responsibility was given to the older sibs to buy any necessary food which they could do on credit by signing a "tick". Don recalled Malama's Grocery Store and Chick's Deli where we could buy a variety of fresh foods and "The Spaghetti Inn' on the other corner where a warm meal could be purchased for some or all of the family.

Dad would struggle with two promises that he had made to our mom before she died: that he would not remarry and that the children would not again be sent back to an institution like the orphanage

Mother's death was "a major calamity for all of us" as Ray experienced feeling like he was being "deserted" when he visited mother in the hospital with "various tubes protruding from her arms". (R. Kuby, Chronology p.5). The disappointment was all the worse as she was supposed to be getting better based on small signs of hope (e.g. that she could eat oranges) but then her untreated infection took its toll which later discovered antibiotics could have healed.

Dad had an emotional outburst at the funeral services as he cried out that he didn't want to live any more which was very frightening to Ray and the other children now solely dependent on him. Rita, the eldest in the family, "cried hysterically as mother's body was lowered into the grave" in sharp contrast to the priest's prayers of faith for an afterlife. Rather than faith, Ray chose the "sad realism" that "when you die, you are (simply) dead" which Ray says that he felt "at some deep level" at this very sad event. (ibid. p. 5)

Tom described our mother's death as our family's greatest sorrow during this five year period. The family all gathered around our mother's deathbed at St. Anne's hospital on February 23,1942, as mother said her farewell. She would die at the young age of 36 after giving births to seven children with the eighth being the stillbirth, named Theresa. Our mother is remembered by Tom as a **woman "with boundless energy, joy, self-sacrifice, love, kindness and deep religious faith."** (TK, Our Journey, 5/1996).

Despite our dad's deep expression of grief at the death of our mom, Ray was impressed that our dad showed discipline in continuing both his manual labor and taking over mother's work of shopping, cooking and childcare no matter how he felt This continuity of care after so great a loss was reassuring to all the dependent children.

Our dad soon realized that he couldn't do both his work and that of our now missing mother. At the young age of 14, our sister Jane decided to take over our mother's childcare and housework. Jane's early choice probably saved me from potential trauma over the loss of a mother at the vulnerable age of only two. **Jane** was the earliest of my heroes who **combined hard work with a responsible, loving relationship.** Jane's love would need to be balanced with assertiveness over time as she needed to convince dad to hire a part-time house keeper to make her excessive work load manageable.

Dennis would be an important brother for both Ray and David at the family's first real home in Wade Park on the East side of Cleveland. At 12, Dennis began collecting money during the war to "buy bombs for MacArthur". From this money, Dennis purchased a General MacArthur's uniform for David which had the power to stop the busy traffic outside our home just as David raised his hand wearing his power clothes. The traffic would stop because Dennis would see when the light would turn red before sending David out into the traffic. Unfortunately, one day David decided to put on his General MacArthur uniform by himself and try crossing the street without Dennis. Dennis watched from the house in anguish as David walked out in the rush hour traffic without observing the changing of the light to red. The traffic did stop without running over David, but that would be the last time that he would see his General MacArthur uniform as it would now be burned to avoid a repeat of David walking out into traffic.

Dennis claimed that he was "unilaterally assigned" to watch over his younger brother so that check ins with the older sibs would also be "Hi Dennis where's David?" Dennis took his responsibility seriously to the point where he got Ray to agree to include David on park hikes and street car rides to see war movies.

World War II provided double shifts for dad which allowed him the sufficient income to feed seven children and pay the rent of our downstairs house. When the war ended, the family celebrated the victory of our allies over the evil dictatorships in Germany and Japan. Unfortunately, the war's end meant a radical decrease in hours and income for our dad leading to an eviction from our Wade Park home. Both Rita and Jane would marry Vets returning from active combat. Don and Tom would enter the seminary in Pennsylvania to complete their high school education and give them chances to become priests. The three youngest brothers, Ray, Dennis and David, would be sent to live with an uncle and an aunt in Johnstown.

9.5—Resilience and Reunion in Johnstown as Wade Park Ends

After the family's eviction from Wade Park, Ray and Dennis were challenged to adjust to life with unknown relatives in Johnstown (**Photo #5**)**.** In retrospect, Ray concluded that Dennis 'grasped the new social

THE HEROIC RESILIENCE OF HAPPINESS

situation in Johnstown correctly" with his "emotional intelligence" in contrast to Ray's rebellions which made Ray's short 10 month stay with a "one-way bus ticket back to Cleveland."

In a short story (The House on the Hill") Ray described the idealized version given to them by our brother Don of how "wonderful their new life would be in Johnstown" which led to Ray's disappointments, rebellion and eventual "eviction" from Johnstown before his first year was completed there. Consider the following differences between Don's idealized vision contrasted the reality. Who were these relatives with whom the brothers were going to stay for an unknown period? Don seemed to have the inside answers to every possible question to provide positive motivations for this big change.

"Mary was a typical Irish Colleen born in County Mayo, a Boyle by birth whose uncle was the Bishop of Pittsburgh...and a professional nurse. John was a Police Captain in the main police district in Johnstown. They lived in a huge house, on top of one of the seven hills overlooking the city of Johnstown… with Sean their beautiful Irish Setter..and uncle John's black Roadster in which he took such pride in keeping it in top condition." Don's stories had made this move easier to take and Ray began to look forward to his new home with the Colleen and the Captain.

This first shock was that the Colleen was very **overweigh**t, elderly and not attractive. The second surprise was that the boys were to go home on a **street car.** "You mean you don't even have a car!" The next question was where was the police station where John was **Captain** to which Mary answered with the question: "Where did you get all this nonsense? John has been working for the fire department for the past 27 years. Ray didn't hide his disappointment and vowed to get even with Don for all the "nonsense" he gave causing such a bad first impression. Still Ray had to ask one last question for his own satisfaction: "Where was the beloved Irish Setter?" To which Mary answered, "I don't like dogs and neither does your uncle John and we have never had a dog in our lives." (ibid.)

With so many illusions shattered, it was no surprise that Ray at 15 could not fit into the realities of the home where he had been placed. Ray's emergent new value system was not compatible either with John in Johnstown or with our dad in Cleveland. As a resilient teen, he would have to find his own independence no matter what the challenges were to be overcome.

On the other hand, Dennis showed some "social intelligence" in adapting to Johnstown made easier by his business skills to make a name for himself as Mr. Baseball I.Q. when he worked as a moving snack vendor at Johnstown baseball games. Dennis would challenge potential customers to ask him any question they wanted about baseball. If Dennis answered their question correctly, they would be obliged to buy a snack at cost or if he failed they would get a snack free. As his time showed, Dennis rarely failed to deliver and gained a popular reputation.

As Dennis earned money from this job, he would enjoy his role as the "big brother" proudly jingling the money in his pockets while giving David balloons and small treats. He was also the IQ guy in Science showing off his knowledge by answering any Science question David could ask.

Ray had already returned to Cleveland before the family celebration of David's first communion. Dennis was present as were Tom and Don since they were seminarians in a nearby town of Holdaysburg, a short ride east of Johnstown. In this context, having two potential priests show up for a religious rite of passage magnified the spiritual power of this day. **(Photo #6)**.

Dennis later chose to return to Cleveland when he was old enough to take care of himself since our father worked night hours and slept during the day. Like Ray, Dennis had to switch to public schools since parochial schools were either too expensive or beyond walking distance. When Dennis returned to Cleveland, Ray was no longer living with Dad but living independently and working a couple after-school jobs to pay for his rent after his fall-out with Dad around differences in religion.

I began to see that our home with extended relatives was conditional and I had concerns that I too could get sent back if I rebelled as Ray had and allowed my anger to be expressed disrespectfully. Ray was competent to cope at 15 but at the age of nine, I became anxious that I would be alone as dad worked and would be unable to make it as Ray did finding his own place to live, finding odd jobs to do to support himself and managing his studies by himself without adult help. My aunt helped assure me that I was loved as if I were her real child.

Although we did not fully appreciate this Mary at the time, she was a hero for taking on the burden of three unknown nephews at her advanced age and poor health. Ray and Dennis were returned to our original hometown of Cleveland after short stays, but I was able to stay on from first grade through the end of 9th grade with some positive benefits. The times were changing quickly for my brothers while I was still in the midst of my childhood.

9.6—Military, Marriage and Adult Careers for Older Sibs.

After a few years, both of the seminarian brothers developed an interest in the opposite gender which didn't fit in with their requirements for celibacy needed to become priests. Soon after both Don and Tom left their seminary for secular lives only to get another "calling" for a lifestyle change. This time it was the draft board that called both brothers to serve in the military during the Korean "conflict". Ray had already enlisted and ended up in Germany with Tom where they both did office work for their entire time of military duty. Don was drafted into the infantry and ended up in actual combat near the DMZ battling North Korea. Don sustained physical injuries and emotional trauma requiring hospitalization followed by an honorable discharge.

The gap between my brothers and I was growing large. A photo shows three brothers in the military in their 20's while I was a Boy Scout at 11-12 (**Photo #7**). After his three years as a soldier in Germany, Ray went to Antioch College where he met his future wife, Alma. Ray and Alma were married in October of 1955 in White Plains, New York. In the process, Ray converted to Judaism to join Alma's faith community. Don had already converted to Judaism in order to marry his Jewish wife, Ruth, and was able to be Ray's best man in the wedding.

After graduating from Antioch, Ray would go on to the University of Chicago Law School to become a lawyer. Both Ray and Dennis moved from their origins in poverty to professional careers in the upper middle class. Ray recalled reading about a middle class family in elementary school in a book called "Dick and Jane" which described an enviable lifestyle at the time from Ray's perspective. This ideal middle class family owned their own home in a safe neighborhood, had a family car, a dog, a cat and just two kids, Dick and Jane (until Sally came along later). Order would produce wealth and wellbeing!

While in college, Dennis worked in the home of Dr. Gresham, President of Bethany College who inspired him to pursue a career in the ministry. Dennis had a brief training period as a Marine but was released when the hardships of basic training created a medical condition which disqualified him as a full Marine yet satisfied his military requirements. Dennis would follow his mentor into divinity school training to become a Unitarian minister following his sales job in Erie where he met his future wife, Jeanne. Their wedding in June 1960 would be a happy occasion for our family reunion. Soon after, Dennis would enter a Unitarian seminary graduating just as their son Scott was born. Dennis would then begin a well-publicized career (again seizing opportunities) as a Unitarian minister in the inner city of Cleveland which included marches with Dr. Martin Luther King. After receiving many death threats by phone and mail, Dennis would take on another congregation in the valley suburbs of Los Angeles. Finally, he would come to Berkeley where he stayed for the rest of his life. He worked for Starr King Unitarian grad school and led groups into parks to experience "God in Nature" as part of his ecological activism. Always a good salesman, Dennis found a better income than he had in ministry by selling life insurance whose target speciality was wealthy doctors.

Both Tom and Don corrected the mistakes of their hasty first marriages (Joan and Ruth) in finding lasting, satisfying remarriages, Tom to Barb, and Don to Lolette. Barb later chose to convert to Judaism and Tom joined her. From his successful career in public relations, Tom would have monthly newsletters about the family, promote periodic reunions and make films of significant events like weddings thus generously filling a fatherly (or Patriarchal) role for our family through his artistic talents and his ability to capture news that made each of us feel appreciated.

David was a full decade behind three of his brothers as they served in the military, graduated from college and married while David was still a child of ten in 1950 and just 13 when Ray, 9 years older, finished his three years of service and began his college degree at Antioch where he would meet his wife, Alma.

9.7- My Resilience through Mentors in Johnstown & Cleveland

While the brothers grew from the responsibility of military service, I was to progress toward maturity from my Scouting mentor, Ed Davis, who combined the rigors of Scout training with a Methodist warmth and conversational prayer which would become a supplement to the formality and ritual prayers of Catholicism.

Scouting allowed me to become closer to nature camping out for weekends or longer during all the four seasons, esp. cold in the Pennsylvania winters and full of flowers and animals in spring and summer. Meeting weekly provided me with another community different from my parochial school friends, mainly Protestant rather than Catholic, but with varying degrees of genuine faith and prayer. My Scout community gave me stability as the health of my aunt was failing. My aunt Mary died in mid-June just after the completion of seventh grade when I was thirteen years old. Despite her ill health, I came to realize that she was the leader of our family who kept us functional. With Mary gone, uncle John and I were like two bachelors picking up the loose ends of cooking, cleaning and clothes shopping as we went along. Although a hero as a Veteran and Fireman, John could not help me with my school work in eighth or ninth grades. After returning to Cleveland, I found that my dad could do no better in academics than my uncle and that I was pretty much on my own with school.

Just as my sister **Jane** stepped in as my mentor and hero to spare me from the devastation of losing my mother at the age of two, now a "sister" of a different kind, a nun named **Sister Carolyn** was my 8th grade teacher who was truly a hero in every sense of the word - caring, concerned but disciplined and fair. Sister Carolyn challenged me to bring out a diverse set of talents that I never knew I had, ranging from acting in plays to spontaneous comedy, as the class reviewed the weekly news. Not only was my grief given relief but my self-confidence was restored to inspire my highest level of performance that allowed me into the gifted class of scholars in my first year in High School. I am shown at the end of 8th grade grade joyously throwing my books up in the air symbolizing the success fostered by Sister Carolyn. A photo of our music teacher in eight grade shows the habit which Sister Carolyn wore in her order (St. Joseph). **(Photo #8)** Sister Carolyn's photo is not available but she looked like the nun played by Ingrid Bergman in the 1944 nostalgic movie, *"The Bells of St. Mary's."*

In our year book of 1954, was this photo of our gifted class including two of my best friends, Jackie Bifano and Bob Vranka. This 9th grade had been the high point of my school community just as 8th grade had been the high point of my grief recovery through the mentoring work of Sister Carolyn. (**Photo #9**)

After that academic peak year would come a period of the pits where I would be taken out of my compatible community to join a new school as an unwelcome outsider worthy of scorn and derision. Since my aunt had died, my older brothers thought that it would be best to have me join my family in Cleveland and attend a public school. I was coming from a small town to a city from a small school to a big school and coming from a community centered on religion to one that was totally secular. I thought that joining the brothers would be a homecoming but my brothers were either away in college, in their careers and busy with their own families. I lived with my dad in the inner city who worked all night long making airplane parts and sleeping most of the day before he returned to work again following a long bus ride. Neither my dad or my uncle had graduated from high school, so my academic work was all mine to work through. The worst of my public school experiences was the informal practice of "mocking" anyone who was different in any way such as being from a different country, a different state or a different junior high school. Whenever I raised my hand to contribute ideas, I could hear Ken Mc. and his allies in the back of the room "mocking" me by imitating me to produce ridiculing humor at my expense. The irony was that I found myself happy to eat lunch with those who were rejected such as the Polish, Chinese, Lithuanian immigrants who seemed to me more interesting and kind than the group doing the rejection. This experience was a step in appreciating "diversity" which would eventually lead me to degrees in Cultural Anthropology

Amidst the mocking, I found myself being encouraged by our literature teacher, Ms. Janet W., who seemed like Sister Carolyn, both in bringing forth my talents while maintaining a disciplined balance with our class. Once again I found a resilience that would lead me to new responsibilities as President of the College Club, some acting, some choir, getting better grades and, to my surprise, being admitted to the National Honor Society. All of the above helped me get admitted to the college of my choice which has both a work/study) "co-op" program and the third year optional study in Europe The pits of high school helped me into the peaks of college fulfillment. A side note was that an essay that I wrote claiming that Jesus was a myth (inspired by my brother Don) led to weekly conversations on the historical truth of Christ with the balance which I have seen with Catholics who are confident in their truth without any bullying or emotionality. Ms. Janet W. and I would exchange Christmas cards for a half century as I regained my faith. **(Photo #10)**

9.8— Spiritual Resilience in College and Work

I had followed Ray's recommendation to attend his college where co-op job experience was had every year connected to one's major. One of my co-op jobs early in my Antioch career was working for the Naval Research Labs in Washington, D.C. From this location, I would make it to Erie, PA for the wedding of my brother Dennis when I was 20 and finally reaching an equity of height with my brothers. **(Photo #11)**.

So much as Antioch was a wonderful fit, but my conservative (Catholic) conscience and Antioch's liberalism would collide when I became a hall advisor. The freshmen who were assigned to my guidance wanted to enjoy the opportunity of co-ed camping out in "Glen Helen" where there was no supervisor. One nineteen year old freshman from my Hall got his girlfriend pregnant while camping in the Glen. The girl's parents were irate and forced them into a marriage for which neither was mature enough to sustain. I became anxious about sexual choices outside my control for which I felt responsible and went into the pits of a depression, couldn't concentrate on my studies and was on the verge of poor grades. The co-op system brought me resilience through "work therapy" which began after Christmas at a reading clinic in Pontiac Michigan helping teens who were struggling with their own academic failings.

My female boss was experienced with the psychological side of her high school students failing in school and became a mentor for me. She began giving me simple jobs and praised me for doing them right, Gradually she increased what I was expected to do and I was amazed that I could now do what I couldn't do at the outset of my job. Within the three month job period, I experienced the resilience of going from the pits as a very depressed, struggling person into the peaks of becoming a competent and confident person. When I returned to campus for the Spring quarter, I was inspired to take on many new challenges with confidence and success for my best academic output and fulfillment to that point. The familiar pattern repeated itself again as a mentor helped me find my resilience from the losing pits to the winning peaks.

My last co-op job would be a year long in Los Angeles, CA which extends beyond my graduation working with brain-injured and/or emotionally disturbed children under an eccentric genius born in Austria, Marianne Frostig. I roomed with Nick G. for the most satisfying two years of independent living, joy and freedom. At the end we both took a student ship to Europe for a year. We both became therapists after studying in other fields -Nick in Linguistics) and I in World religions..

My MA paper in world religions was on the Swazi as I graduated from Divinity School at the University of Chicago. I sent this paper to a specialist in Swazi religion at UCLA, Dr. Hilda Kuper, who cleared the way for me to become her doctoral student in Anthropology. Dr. Kuper would write the biography of *King Sobuza (**Photo #12**), the longest reigning monarch in Southern Africa. In order to be prepared for my fieldwork in the remote areas of Swaziland, I trained with the Peace Corps to improve my language skills which involved living with a Swazi family who spoke no English. I would later stay with Peace Corps volunteers stationed as teachers all over the country to study the interactions of Christianity with the indigenous culture. Seen in a photo are my main contacts from the Peace Corps and the University for Swazi students where I taught for two years after my year of full time research. Up until this time, at 36 I was still a student, unmarried, not yet settled down as I prepared to return to the USA to write up the results of my field work for my PhD dissertation. Only after my doctorate was completed did normal adult life begin for me with marriage and decade long jobs on a career track.

9.9— Resilience and Mentors in My Career and Marriage

Over our adult lives, religion had remained important to my family as a whole. The brother closest to my age, Dennis, became a Unitarian minister and the next older brother, Raymond became Jewish by marriage and a lawyer by profession. Not only did I follow Ray to his Alma Mater, Antioch, but I went on to follow him to the University of Chicago for a graduate degree in Divinity Studies which led me to my years of fieldwork in Africa and my own conversion. Later I would teach at a Christian college for a decade, helped by mentors and companions on my journey. Although Ray and I shared so much background of family and two universities, we were opposites as to religious and political views since he was a liberal Reformed Jew and I was a conservative Catholic. Nevertheless, Ray and I enjoyed a close friendship and respect for each other beyond the gaps. Ray had more in common with Dennis in their political and religious orientations.

I had models of deep and sincere faith over my entire life from my mother through teaching mentors. Finally I was ready for marriage and a career which would continue the mix of Charismatic spontaneity and Catholic ritual shared by spiritual companions as I approached forty (a late bloomer but still growing!)

My first wife, Jan, the mother of Rebekah and Beth, had a spiritual conversion to Christianity out of Hinduism. As I did the write-up of my fieldwork. My head was full of theory which I allowed to flow out thinking that this could make a positive impression on someone also completing her doctoral research. I was wrong. I reminded her of the egotism of her first husband and she did not want to repeat this mistake. Nevertheless, we were both drawn to a Charismatic Catholic Church (Holy Redeemer) which we attended every Friday night long enough to renew rather than end our relationship. We would later be married at Holy Redeemer after becoming part of a live in-staff who were to be leaders of monthly healing retreats **(Photo #13)** and have our two daughters four years apart.

Jan taught Microbiology at San Francisco State from which post she created successful textbooks used widely in the USA and abroad. Jan would advance up her career ladder to provide a sufficient income for our family of four.

As early as 1990, Jan was afflicted with breast cancer which would eventually lead to a double mastectomy which later spread to become uterine cancer. Jan's religious search became deeper and longer bringing resilience to her long battle with cancer but one week she suddenly became weaker going into a bed from which she would not raise herself. She would die August 17, 1996 but the light which filled her eyes showed that she was lifted up given witness by a praying Christian who had a vision which she shared. **(Photo #14)**. Jan would leave a legacy of her popular text books on Immunology which would live on for over a decade providing income for the remaining family of three.

Jan's death was a great loss to our family. Our 15 year old, Rebekah, was having a hard time in school despite the school changes which I made and was drawn to friends who were rebels. Beth at 11 surrounded herself with good friends (as was her norm) and join a variety of athletic teams with her friends (soccer, softball, volleyball) which were easy for me to support with regular attendance and enthusiastic cheering.

I had a private practice in counseling out of a church in Fairfield beginning in 1991 when I received my MFT license validating an independent business. In 1994, a family came to me to work through a major transition of their daughter.

I was so impressed by the power of the Charismatic prayers of the mother, Gail, that I began to seek her help for prayer support with other clients. I had long realized that successful counseling required a prayer group and was happy to hear that Gail was the leader of an active prayer group, mentored by Roy & Mickey Pearson, and would even be available to pray in session with particular clients. I no longer required supervision but having a second, insightful opinion on clients was essential for my work.

Gail provided new perspectives from her feminine intuition and training as a nurse. Both of these perspectives were helpful as Gail joined me in sessions with difficult clients who had suffered from traumatic circumstances. Gail and I worked as clinical colleagues but both of us also needed time to process issues with our children who were going through some hard times. Sharing our spirituality, the counseling work and our own issues became a main source of support for me as Jan's breast cancer metastasized into uterine cancer. Jan had known how disabling my dad's promise to our mom home was to never remarry and she did not want that void either for me or our two daughters. At this point, I was far from imagining Gail as a future wife but we each provided the mutual support we both needed as each of us struggled with different family issues.

With some female clients (and even co-workers), male therapists need to have clear, consistent boundaries to manage romantic transference issues. I knew that I had to set clear limits with some few of my female clients, but Gail was very balanced and grounded in her energy and our support was not one-sided. Furthermore, Gail had a deep Catholic spirituality and was committed to her marriage. Our relationship grew over the course of our first year working together and we began to experience depths we had longed for which our marriage circumstances were not allowing. All of our meetings were covered with sincere prayer seeking discernment and direction. Neither of us would allow any sexual expression but we were having levels of closeness which some would call "an affair of the heart" (and mind but not body). Soon a separation would occur as Jan's cancer worsened leading to a sudden death in mid-August 1996. I would close down my Fairfield practice to be at home with my two teenaged daughters and did little counseling for the rest of 1996.

As much as I tried as a father, I knew that my daughters needed a mother's experience and guidance both in the practical needs of clothes shopping and in the emotional needs to be heard from the heart by a mom substitute.

Within six months, Gail began coming down to console the grief in my family as part of her **"Faith in Action**" ministry which she had begun with nine other nurses. We needed a new beginning before the end of the first year of Jan's death. One way to start over again was to take my daughters to the two places responsible for my conversion Israel and Africa. Our church was sponsoring a ten day trip to Israel and Gail was able to book the last opening with her husband Tom. In Israel, we were able to grieve and make a new beginning after some deep spiritual experiences which Gail shared. **(Photo #15)**. The wailing wall was a symbol that the pits of grief could be consoled through a resilience into a new life. **(Photo #16)** After Israel, my two daughters and I went to Swaziland in Africa where I had studied the resilience of conversion for

3 years and made my rebirth into Catholicism which was both deeply familiar and emotionally new. Our grief as a family was being healed.

Upon her return from Israel, Gail spent six weeks with her brother who was dying from pancreatic cancer. We had become a mutual support couple through the healing work we had done for others, and now we could help each other through a new source of grief. Eight years after Jan's death in mid-1996, we found ourselves ready for marriage in 2004 after much time in spiritual direction and prayer since we found ourselves deeply in love and soulmates.

Three years later we would have our marriage blessed in the Catholic Church.

At the age of 64, I began a new life with a new wife (**Photo #17**) as celebrated by my four brothers (and their wives). A symbol of our new blended family were Gail's three daughters (Molly, Amy. Laura) joining with the Kuby two daughters (Beth and Rebekah). Gail's son, Jon, would walk her down the aisle to affirm her transition into a new marriage. **(Photo #18)**. Also active in our wedding were the twins of Amy, Mia and Greg, along with Jon's child, Brook. Two other grandchildren (Zosia and Hannah) were absent but symbolically represented. (**Photo #19**). Once a year family from out of town would join the local family in family celebrations as seen in a photo gathering which includes Rebekah (with Alan a longtime friend), Laura and her husband Gordy. **(Photo #20.)**

Faith requires a shared community and the Thompson family has been our mix of a consistent extended family community over a twenty year period since the birth of their twins, Mia and Greg **(Photo #21)** from Thanksgiving through Christmas unto Easter and birthdays/anniversaries. Although Gail had a divorce, Tom continues to be a consistent part of every family gatherings over an 18 year period showing grace of forgiveness over this major change. Molly usually joins our seasonal gatherings.

Gail and I would become active in another faith community as we began teaching in the Christian College of Patten in 2005 for the next nine years. About the same time Gail became active in another faith community as she joined the choir at Lourdes. Music has been a deep love in Gail's life for most of our 18 years of marriage. Music had been a passion in Gail's family with both her brother and sister being professional pianists and piano teachers following the career of their mother, Alice Schindler and her father's expertise with the violin I share in Gail's love of music and support her music ministry both at Lourdes and up at Fairfield where she provided music for the Sunday Mass once a month for most of two decades.

In addition to music, another of Gail's lifelong loves has been children. When her daughter Amy had twins of Mia and Greg, she worked with them for four years and then was referred to another family with the twins of Zach and Nate. She became "hooked on twins" and has now been with Zach and Nate for sixteen years while adding a new family when Jasper was born (not a twin but a referral from the parents of Zach and Nate) to a mom who specialized in autism (which Zach had). We continue to share the lives of our twins, Mia and Greg, now 20 and half way through college. **(Photo #22)**.

Gail has actively joined me as a co-grandparent for the two latest grandchildren of daughter Beth and Pete Camou. Gail has a special love for young children like Sophie (**Photo #23**) and John David. (**Photo #24**)

The faith shared by Gail and David has been important as they have watched the deaths of family members. Gail lost both her brother Frank and her mother to Pancreatic cancer within a two year period. Gail's training and experience as a nurse allowed her to help her brother Frank in his year long battle with cancer and especially during the last six weeks of his life when his health declined dramatically to die at the young age of 58. By contrast, Gail's mother, Alice, would die at an advanced age of 96 from a similar diagnosis. Both Frank and Alice would continue their passions and skill for music until the end of their lives. Gail's last remaining sib, Laura, continues to be a piano teacher for high-achieving children and young adults. This book has focused on the Kuby family. To do justice to Gail's resilience on the Schindler side would require a new book.

The death of Jesus was followed by the ultimate resilience of His Resurrection three days later. His death gave us full forgiveness from our repented sins and his resurrection shows that we will all be victorious over death. God's spiritual victory has "already" happened but our spiritual victory over death is "not yet". We live between the gaps of our future resurrection and present journey through our increasing mortality. God can seem faraway at times, but every experience of RESILIENCE in our lives is a tangible touch of Christ's resurrection power.

Our resilience is helped by our mentors and companions on our journey through the ups and downs of life who affirm with that God is bigger than every form of dying or tragic loss.

Theologians tell us that we have three different kinds of spiritual battles throughout our lives: the flesh, the world and the devil. First, we battle different forms that our "flesh" vulnerability to sin can take. Second, we battle our elitist culture which brings the power of the group and ideology to ridicule and undermine our faith by claiming a higher authority of science. Third, we have the invisible spirit of evil itself always in disguise and acting remotely. We have seen undisguised evil in the face of Putin as he destroys vulnerable civilian centers of hospitals, schools, homes. We can pray, contribute money and keep abreast of the news of the suffering in Ukraine as we await God's power for resilience, recovery and resurrection. As a form of prayer for hope, we must each practice the virtues which bring resilience and heroism into our lives inspired by their great heroism and sacrifice of those good people fighting evil.

We must all battle the power of sin through transparency before God, the humble admission of character flaws and seeking to know God's love above the accusations and condemnation of all false gods. We need praying faith communities grounded in the truth to confront false ideologies which justify various forms of mob rule, violence, and lies. Finally we need to know and see how the devil operates in our day through the deadly Fentanyl drug now coming across our border via China and the Mexican cartels which exploit desperate poor people. We must be part of functional and effective communities who can show that truth outlasts lies, that love is stronger than hate and that faith brings resilience from every defeat, loss or setback.

9.10—The Resilience of Faith and the Family Bonds of Love

Just as we began our story with our family just coming into its full membership (as our sunrise), we now end our story with the last full gathering (minus Rita and Don) of our family core (2004 on) as we move toward our sunsets. We see our family gathering of four brothers and their four wives raising their toasts celebrating the joy of our reunion **(Photo #25)**.

THE HEROIC RESILIENCE OF HAPPINESS

In the far left we see Ray and Alma. Ray continues with clarity of mind and health at 90 but his wife Alma died of Pancreatic cancer at 88 seemingly waiting until the day of their 66 anniversary before passing on 10/22/21. Ray's son Michael lives nearby and is very involved in supporting Ray with daily meals and walks. Eric goes back and forth between Chicago and California where he has just become a grandfather for the third time to Nora, daughter of Alex and Joanna. Eric has three adult children, Alex, Michelle and Brooke.

Next is the very tall Dennis with his very short wife Jeanne. Dennis died peacefully in a rest home from unknown causes at the age of 84 in April of 2019 within days of Easter and Passover. His wife Jeanne outlived him by three years but, as she told her niece, "My castle is crumbling, Lamb chop!" Jeanne died in April of 2022 having lived a full life until 96. The ashes of both Dennis and Jeanne have been sent to Erie to be buried in the Benedict family plot of Jeanne's wealthy adopted parents who raised her.

Tom, the creative patriarch, and his wife Barb are next. Tom died at 87 leaving his wife, younger by a decade, to grieve the loss of such a fulfilling marriage and rich lifestyle of travel, art and music. In his obituary of 2014, Tom is remembered someone both "impish and elegant" who "exuded energy in life" with "creativity as a defining feature of his entire life" from teaching creativity to scientists and engineers to his becoming an accomplished artist. (Plain Dealer).

Gail and I are last on the right. Except for us, only two (Ray & Barb) remain with four having passed over (Alma, Dennis, Jeanne & Tom). Missing are the two sibs who died a decade or more before, Rita, Don and his wife Lola. Spending holidays with Don and Lola had been rich and rewarding.

What we have from our love for each other over the past are are joyful and cherished memories. We now carry our love and experience into the unknown future dedication to our grandchildren. We have shared a full 20 years close-up with Mia and Greg and now we enjoy the new Camou grandchildren (Sophie and John) across the miles. Other grandchildren seen less often because of distance are Hannah, Brook, and Zosia but in our hearts and prayers.

The lifespan lessons described by Erik Erikson indicate that the last stage of life is a time of "reviewing our lives" with both positive cherished memories and sometimes painful reminders of past mistakes. Resilience uses the positivity of peaks to lift our spirits out of the negativity of the pit periods of our lives, long or short.

Facing the pits of life, such as the deaths of loved ones, a balancing resilience is sought. Our resilience in life is our foreshadowing of the resurrection of all the beloved lost to death and a future joyful reunion where the pits of death and loss are are transformed by the peaks of life in an eternal presence of an ultimate Loving God. The gap between the challenges of earth and the fulfillments of heaven seem great because God is invisible and can seem absent. So where is the God whom the Bible claims is omnipresent and therefore always close to us?

Both Gail and I have known God early in our lives through loving families who sought God's holy presence and will. We have both experienced the "pits" of losing beloved family but we have both learned to seek and find peaks of renewal through the power of spiritual resilience. We both seek the stable balance between the ups and downs of life but increasingly see God's presence in both the pits and the peaks. in every resilience, we have come slowly to see every pit as God's call to reach out for help wherein trust replaces my anxiety or anger. Our resilience prayer is "Jesus we trust in you" followed by celebrations of gratitude for being lifted up out of life's down times. We thank God for the beloved mentors and companions of our lives for their guidance on this shared journey as we now celebrating the challenges of being "elders" together with God's love and faithfulness.

CHAPTER TEN

THE RESILIENT POWER OF FAITH AND FAMILY

Illustrations of our Biographical Overview

#1—Our parent's wedding: Mary Ann & Paul 1924

*#2—Seven sibs together at Orphanage 1940: (left to right.)
Dennis, Jane, Don, Mom holding David, Tom, Rita, Ray.*

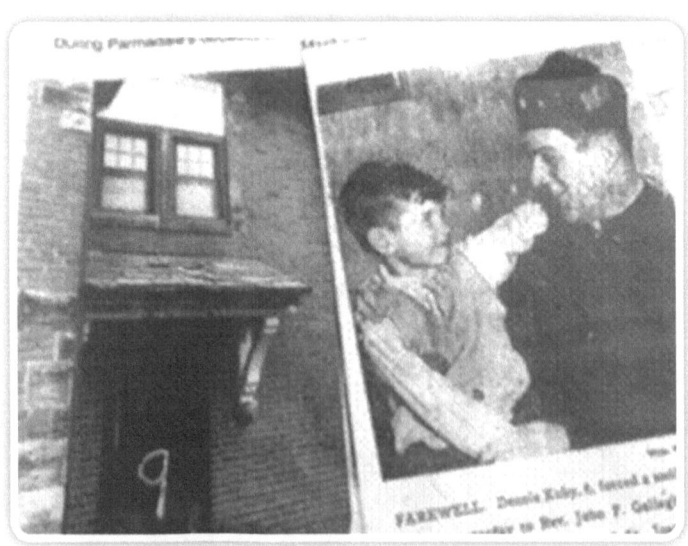

#3—Orphan cottage and Dennis says goodbye to Father Gallagher

#4—Jane and her 3 brothers (Dennis, Ray, David) on 7009 Wade Park Porch. After our mom's death in 1942, our first home together.

#5—Three youngest brothers: L to R: Ray, David, Dennis in their new home in Johnstown 1946 with Dad's older brother John.

#6—Two Seminarian brothers (Tom & Don) join Dennis for David's First Communion. L to R: Dennis, Tom, Aunt Mary, Don with David in front.

#7—above image shows Tom, Don & Ray ((L to R). in Korean War 1950-52 Bottom image shows David in Scouts 1952. A decade behind

#8—Celebrating a year of success thanks to Sister Carolyn's mentoring June 1954 after grief following the death of my aunt Mary June 1953. (Photo is of Music teacher, Sr. Robert).

#9—Ninth Grade Honors Class '54-'55 with no bullies and the most interesting bright students city-wide. (David in front row for short people, only half class pictured.)

#10—Ms. Wiley restores self-esteem from 10th grade bullies in a Cleveland Public school & helps my success for admission to Antioch.

#11—Dad and five sibs at Dennis/JB wedding in Erie 1960 where I finally grow up to my brothers' height at age 20. Dad, David, Ray, Tom, Don & Dennis (left to right.)

#12—Three years research & teaching in Africa connected to Peace Corps friends. (David, King Sobhuza photo, Beth, Isa, Ray & Irene.) Peace Corps required living with rural Swazi families for 3 months to learn the language to which I joined to make valuable connections & friends.

#13—My Marriage to Janis Mower resulting in Beth, Rebekah daughters

Beth and Rebekah with parents six years later.

#14—Jan dies on August 17, 1996 Through Jesus the Holy Lamb of God. A Love stronger than death at only 49 years of age after completing a successful textbook on Immunology.

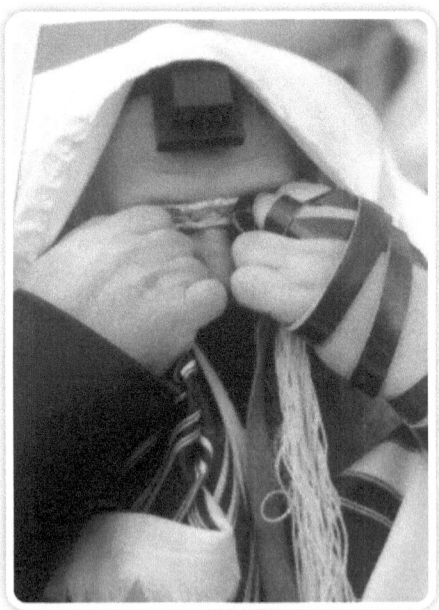

#15—Trip with daughters to Jerusalem in 1996, grief comforted by Gail. (Left to right, David, Gail and fellow pilgrim)

#16—Wailing Wall in Jerusalem Where Jews mourn the loss of the Temple.

#17—Celebration of marriage to Gail with Amy behind and the four Kuby brothers (left to right.) David, Ray, Dennis, & Tom, the best man. 7/31/04

#18—The creation of a blended family with five daughters: Beth, Rebekah, Molly, Amy and Laura (left to rt.) around the groom David and bride Gail.

#19—The young grandchildren added: left to rt. Hannah. Zosia, Greg, Jon holds Brook & Gail holds Mia.

#20—Extended blended family holiday gathering with out-of-towners Gordy &Laura, Rebekah & Alan and the local Thompsons & Molly. 2010

#21—The four Thompsons, Mia, Greg, Amy & Mike in middle. 2015

#22—Two sets of twins: Mia & Greg, Nate & Zach, and two young sibs, Ellison & Jasper, Gail in middle. 2023

#23—Beth Kuby Camou with Sophie. 2019

#24—Pete Camou with John. 2021

#25—Four brothers and wives give a goodbye toast and blessing: Ray, Alma, Dennis, Jeanne, Barb & Tom, and David with Gail. 2010

PREFACE #1—
WHY IS THIS BOOK IS NEEDED?

The short answer is to help us realize that we are all on the Titanic with its wonderful technology and excellent cuisine but destined to an ending beyond the control of its passengers. Yet we have repeated experiences of resilience in our battles with the evil or deadly "pits" of life as previews of our own resurrections and encounters with the divine mercy of a Higher Power to find a deeper truth and meaning in our lives to comfort us in the midst of tragic losses and bring an abiding light during times of darkness. Here is an expanded reflection below.

The thrust of the first half of the lifespan appears that we are getting more powerful and more loving as we grow from early childhood into midlife, but the rise is followed by a decline. We see that our careers often peak at midlife and then decline lower than the state we would wish from the high point of our life and that the physical descent into old age and death looks like we missed the happiness train altogether. Only a minority of life's pilgrims are immortalized through induction into some timeless Hall of Fame or Sainthood while the rest of us live on through the genetic mix of our offspring and largely forgotten in any of the modest career achievements we may have had. However many happy stops we have along life's way, we need to grasp the final destination of this train to have the needed spiritual fitness for this journey.

With our eyes opened to reality, we realize that every "pit" stop of our journey is a preview of our final destiny. Buddhists see each of these "pits" as the "suffering" that comes with our experiential encounters with "impermanence". One remedy is to find ever greater levels of "permanence" with the footsteps of the Buddha as a guide. Christians *understand the "pits" of life as the inevitable small crosses of life before the final cross of death. For both Buddhists and Christians, the pits of life provide a classroom for the development of the spiritual fitness needed to pass the final test to graduate beyond death into eternal life. The big difference is the personal encounter Christians have during their painful crosses as described by Albert Schweitzer. "He comes to us as One unknown...(and) reveals Himself (to both the wise and the simple) in the toils, the conflicts, the sufferings that they shall pass through in His fellowship. And, as an ineffable mystery, they shall learn in their own experience who HE is." (Schweitzer, Quest 1910/98, p.403)*

The Buddhist way follows the impersonal, non-theistic law-based methods of science but the Christian way is "an ineffable mystery" which gives us the intimate compassion of divine "fellowship" with a personal God who "reveals himself to us during our journeys through the pits of frustrating "toils, conflicts, sufferings".

In embracing the cross of Christ, the Christian finds both God's loving forgiveness and resurrection power into eternal life - an offer hard to refuse but it takes "faith". Faith, love, forgiveness and resilience jump out as essentials to the Christian induction into spiritual fitness. The Buddhist virtues of spiritual fitness are complementary in the Christian walk familiar through the detachment and mindfulness required in the twelve step program to become free of the bondage of addictions. The Buddhist path makes a coordinated whole of right thinking, right attitudes, right actions which would lead to the right career and right marriage/ family.

One spectrum of character types as categorized by the Enneagram's nine types has a combination of virtues and vices which require an integration for the authenticity of integrity and coherent wholeness.

Facing the bondage of our vices takes courage, honesty and humility which are the basis of the heroism needed for spiritual fitness. We must battle against our lower self which falls prey to fear, deception and pride. As we seek liberation from the forces that keep us in bondage, we can compensate with the natural virtues of our character type. When our will power fails, we seek a 12 step program that directs us to surrender our false control to our Higher Power above the little addictions that rob our power. Totally ruined lives have been changed from a powerless isolated self to a self empowered by a connection to God as best they can know the intelligent source of power and love in the Universe.

The life span shows the alteration between dependent connection and independent autonomy until there is an integration of the two in the intimate mutuality and greater wholeness of marriage. If we continue this same dynamic in the spiritual realm, our loss of power with age allows us to empower God into our daily lives for a greater intimacy. As our power decreases, God's power increases and we are as connected to God as a baby is to his mother in loving, trusting dependency. Could it be that each of the lifespan tasks challenge us into an installment plan of virtues to prepare us for that final utter dependency of dying to the body to be reborn into a spiritual self? The journey we begin now seeks to answer Zorba when he faced a tragic death: "Where do we come from and where do we go to?"

PREFACE #2— WHAT ARE MY QUALIFICATIONS TO WRITE SUCH A BOOK?

I have been trained in disciplines which try to See Life's Big Map

Religion provides one big map of life as a whole which I learned in nine years of Catholic school education. When I lost my faith orientation to map in my late teens, I went on seek a new map through **philosophy** degree which led me back into religion, all religions this time, specializing in both Buddhism and African religions in graduate school. African religion had to be experienced in community with all of one's senses so I began three years of being immersed in African religious events as an **Anthropologist** to understand both their original religion and the process by which converts came into Christianity with love and power. My immersion into hours of intense Christian worship regained for me the love and power of my original faith map.

I went on to teach from these three big picture perspectives of philosophy, world religions and anthropology both in Africa and the United States for a dozen years. For the last ten years, I added another big picture perspective of studying our resilience through the pits and peaks of our entire lifespan which Erikson divides into eight resilience challenges from birth to death. The book for which this is a preface came into being through as I looked at the big lifespan overview both as a teacher and marriage & family therapist over two decades. In my therapy practice, I see the resilience of couples as they come into my office from their pain in the pits and sooner or later discover the value fo the pits to bring resilience into the higher landscape of living. When

I ask myself how I ever thought that I could do family therapy, I am reminded how I got "drafted" into this job as a child.

As a five year old youngest of seven children, I **learned to listen**. The necessary requirements were to be **unbiased, empathetic, quietly patient** to allow the relief that comes from **being heard from the heart.** In some families, this need was met by the family dog which we couldn't have as renters so I fell into this open job position.

Little did I know that this skill would save me from getting beat up by bullies as I learned to listen, as my family dog role had taught me, to older teens in my class who were now dating girls and having feelings which they needed to talk out to someone with empathy and no judgments.

So it was that my counseling career had been set in motion many years earlier through my survival need to escape harm from older bullies and how could I judge when I was in awe of their humility to reveal their tender side as they pondered the mysteries and miracles of love.

You as the reader might also wonder why and how I became an anthropologist so thanks for asking.

As a child, I had a fascinated interest in Tarzan movies which I would act out in play with peers high up in neighbors' trees. Africa where all types of animals could run free was an experience of paradise lost being regained. My deepest religious longings were met in Africa with charismatic joyful dancing and singing to celebrate both the pits and peaks of life. I would find this joyful form of Christianity back in the USA through the Charismatic renewal in both Catholic and Protestant denominations where I would meet first Jan, the mother of my two daughters, and then Gail, the source of my resilience after the death of Jan.

BIBLIOGRAPHY OF HAPPINESS, HEROISM AND MARRIAGE

(The following books beginning with an asterisk (*) have had the most influence on chapters within of our book.)

1— **Alberti, John, The Working Life, Pearson, NYC, 2004.**

*2— Baron, Renee. and Wagele, Elizabeth, **The Enneagram Made Easy, Harper, San Francisco, 1994.**

*3— **Becker, Ernest, The Denial of Death, Free Press, NYC, 1997.**

4— Cloud, Henry, **Changes that Heal,** Harper, NYC, 1995 and Boundaries in Marriage, Zondervan, Michigan, 1999.

5— Bradshaw, John, **Homecoming: Reclaiming and Healing Your Inner Child, Penquin/Random House, NYC, rev. 1999.**

*6— Brown, Brene, **The Gifts of Imperfection**, Hazelden, Minn. 2010.

7— Buber, Martin, *I and Thou,* Schribner, NYC, 2nd ed. 1958.

8— Campbell, Joseph, **The Hero with a Thousand Faces,** Bollingen, Princeton University, 3rd edition, 1973. (See ref. to Carl Jung)

*9— Carter, B. and McGolderick, M., **The Expanded Family Life Cycle (3rd ed.)** by Pearson Publishing (Allyn & Bacon), Needham Hgts., MA, 2005. (See ch. 15, "Becoming Parents" esp.)

10— Corey, G. *The Theories and Practices of Psychotherapy*, Brooks/Cole, Stamford, CT, 2001. (See chs. 4 Freud, 5 Adler, 6 Existential.

11— Davis, Charles, **"No Key to Happiness"**, Catholic Reporter, 12/15/72, p. 12.

12— Diener, E & R, **Happiness: Unlocking the Mysteries of Psychological Wealth,** Blackwell, Malden, MA, 2008.

13— *Eliade, Mircea, The Sacred and the Profane, Harvest/ Harcourt, NYC, 1959.*

14—Erikson, Erik's **"Psychosocial Theory"** in Boyd, Denise and Bee, Helen, *Lifespan Development,* Pearson/ Allyn & Bacon, NYC, 4th ed. 2006.

15— *Fisher, Mary Pat, Living Religions, Prentice Hall, New Jersey, 6th ed. 2005,(see esp. ch. 5, Buddhism.)*

16— Foster, Richard, **The Celebration of Discipline,** Hodder/ Stoughton, London, Revised 1989.

17— Fromm, Eric, **The Art of Loving,** Harper, NYC, 1956.

18— *Kazantzakis, Nikos, Zorba The Greek, Ballantine, NYC, 1965.*

19— *Jantz, G.L., Happy for the Rest of your Life, Siloam, Florida, 2009.*

20—Kelly, Matthew, **Rediscover Jesus,** Beacon, NYC, 2015.

21— Mandino, Og, **Secrets for Success & Happiness,** Fawcett, 1995.

22— *Mason Mike, The Mystery of Marriage As Iron Sharpens Iron, Multnomah Press, Portland, Ore, 1978.*

23— Moody, Raymond, *Life After Life*, Bantam, NYC, 1975.

24— Powell, John, *Happiness is an Inside Job*, Tabor, CA, 1989.

25— Schweitzer, Albert, *Quest for the Historical Jesus*, John Hopkins Univ. Press, 1910, rev. 1998.

*26— Swmme, Brian & Berry, Thomas, *The Universe Story*, Harper, SF, 1992.

27— Terkle, Studs, *Working*, Labyrinth, NYC, 1997,

28— Tillich, Paul, *The Courage to Be*, Yale, New Haven, 1953.

29— Vann, Gerald, *The Heart of Man*, Doubleday, NY, 1957.

30— Wolfelt, Alan, *Understanding your Grief*, Fort Collin, Colo. 2003.

*31—Williams, Brian, Sawyer, Stacy, Wahlstrom, *Marriage, Families and Intimate Relationships*, Pearson, NYC, 2006. (See chs. 1 happiness, 4 love, 7 marriage, 12 work, research by David Meyers, David Olson, Martin Seligman on our relevant topics.

*32— Yerkovich, Milan & Kay, *How We Love*, Waterbrook, Colo, 2009

33— Kuby, Raymond, **"The House on the Hill"** revised 2020, and **"Safe Haven"**, 3/2/2020.

34— Kuby, Thomas, **"Our Journey for Life's Meaning"**, May 1996.

* * * *

The writer's Example to Illustrate Personalizing the eight chapter topics.

<u>Appendix #1</u>: *Peaks, Pits, Heroes as Children and Teens*

In this section, the writer provides detailed examples from his own journey to stimulate the reader's recall.

a/ Write a letter from your inner child to you as the big sib adult (or parent).

b/ Write a letter back to your inner child with compassion for the child's little power and need for big love and be a channel from your highest self to try and meet the needs of your inner child. Point out when your child's intense emotions try to control your adult better judgment and how the child's wounds or fears can bring out the brat side. Remind the child that adult maturity is a higher authority.

c/ Write a letter from your inner teen to you as the big sib adult (or parent) admitting needs for rebellion, willing to risk confusion and chaos for self-discovery and self realization.

d/ Write a letter back from the adult to the inner teen being compassionate with the teen's rowdiness in seeking autonomy but giving clear messages from the highest, best self for the discipline and balance needed to find middle path between extremes and possible addictions.

e/ What was one major recurrent "pit" during your early childhood that continues to impact the your adult life? What has helped your healing, (author's examples)

f/ What has been a major "peak" or high point in your early life that has had some lasting impact upon you as an adult?

g/ What was a pit of your teen years and how was this helped to impact your adult life in a more positive way?

Appendix #2: The Subjective Dimension of Love and Power in Married Life

a/ What are some memorable or lasting peaks in your marriage or young adult life?

b/ What are some of the peaks and pits of your midlife period?

Appendix #3—Power and Love in Dying and the Afterlife

a/ What are the major challenges (pits) you imagine of your old age?

b/ What are the peaks or hopes you imagine of your senior years"

Appendix #4—Peaks and Pits in Religion and spiritual heroes

a/ What have been some of your negative memories of religion in your life?

What spiritual heroes inspired you during these hard times?

b/ What have been some of the high points of your experience with religion?

What spiritual heroes have been the most influential inspirations of your life.

c/ Do any of the spiritual quotes in this book jump our as relevant to your life.

What spiritual quotes bring the most negative reaction and why?

Appendix #5—Sibling Rivalry, Secure Attachment and Heroes

a/ What are some negative ways (pits) in which you have been impacted by sibling rivalry in your family according to your place of first, last, middle *b/ What has been some positive lasting impacts of sibling relationships in your family as to your position and relationship to your parents?*

<u>Appendix #6</u>—*Enneagram and Balancing Strengths and Weaknesses*

a/ What are some things you like most about one or two of your Enneagram character types as to both strengths and weaknesses?

b/ What are some things that are most difficult, that you like least about your Enneagram character types as to weaknesses and strengths?

<u>Appendix #7</u>—*The Relevance of Happiness Research: Peaks and Pits*

a/ What are some things that make you most Happy (peaks) and what some things that make you most sad (pits) about your set point (genes) or circumstances in your life.

b/ What are somethings that give hope about the happiness research you know? Do you agree that happiness is so little based on circumstances and more on attitude (an inside job)?

<u>Appendix #8</u>—*The Union of Power and Love in Marriage and Family*

a/ What are some ways in which power and love are in conflict in your experience of marriage (your own, parents or sibs")

b/ What integrations have you seen of power and love in marriage that are inspiring and hopeful?

c/ What is one favorite idea from the book (or favorite quote)?

What is your least favorite idea (or quote) from this book.

ENDNOTE

**The Heroic Resilience of Happiness:
Empowered Love thru Life's Pits and Peaks**

According to the research of Erik Erikson, we grow through our human lifespan through **both** the pits and the peaks built into the "crises" of each of our eight stages. Our vision of the peak takes us out of our painful pits to empower us with a love to achieve a resilient "bounce up". This love begins with the mother's love for the helpless baby who just caused the pits of overwhelming birth pains resulting in the miraculous co-creation of another complete human being. The love of our hidden Creator has shown the creative power of His love given tangibly to a loving mother and happy dad. Already in this first stage of life we have both the affirmation and the challenge of our faith. We live in a culture that has had a long Judeo-Christian tradition but we are now increasingly challenged by the secular, scientific world in which we live. We have one companion on each side in ongoing dialogue and debate with us as to the truth which is most sustainable and pragmatic. Each of the two sides have different concepts of the heroism that leads to the Rock of truth (not sinking sand) on which happiness can be securely built. The secular side had no real answer to the grief and loss of loved ones and the anticipation of our own deaths. The heroic virtues which brought me resilience through the losses of my mother as a toddler and my mother-substitute as a teen were the empowering loves of my teen sister and then my 8th grade teacher which took me beyond the pits of grief into a regained happiness.

The secular voices took over for me from 10th grade into college when I lost my faith. The secular world also provided a rich, data-based understanding of world religions which comforted my mind but was not able to restore the deep lost faith of my heart. The contrast was like the stories of two different ships: "The Titanic and "The African Queen". both movies. The secular world produced convincing and logical data along with amazing technology.

The Titanic symbolized the power and grandeur of the secular world: the latest technology and rich, delightful cuisine. The Titanic descended into the deep pit of tragic deaths into the depths of the Ocean. As I write in August o 2023, the "paradise" of key cities on Maui has been totally destroyed by fire. Such a symbol of "paradise lost"!

"The African Queen" was a dilapidated river steamboat owned by a grumpy and alcoholic Charlie (Humphey Bogart) who came to share his boat with a missionary Rose (Katherine Hepburn) following the disaster of a German invasion of the mission in Africa during WW I and the killing of Rose's brother, head of the mission. On "The African Queen", Rose and Charlie would have to survive many challenges from going over raging rapids to being stuck in impenetrable swamps. All the pits and peaks of their voyage together put them in the right place and the right time to destroy an enemy German ship. Enduring their many trials through a love they found for each other gave them the heroic character virtues needed for good to defeat evil and for Charlie to overcome his reliance on alcohol to find courage and comfort. Through love and faith, "The African Queen" began with a tragic death but triumphed where "Titanic failed" relying only on secular technology to overcome death.

As we come into the fragility of our late senior years, "The African Queen" is a symbol of heroically trusting God through all the challenges to our health and the grief of losing dear family members and friends. Unlike those on the Titanic we are not in denial of death and must grow the faith that will make our rebirth more real than death.

Fortunately, the secular and religious truths come closer together through the "Out-of-Body Research done by the center in LA where more than 8 million Americans alone have reported Near Death Experiences (NDE's). Those who return from being seen as "clinically dead", tell similar stories of an overwhelming, unconditional love given by of a "Being of Light" (often seen as Jesus) who reviews their whole lives with a love beyond all judgment giving deep joy and peace despite the realization that these observers are dead and out of their bodies.

This vast amount of empirical data challenges the sufficiency of the materialistic paradigm of secular science showing the need for religious paradigms to be included in our search for truth.

Our "Heroic resilience" through the many pits throughout our lifespan reveals God's inbuilt resurrection power for virtue to prevail over our human weaknesses. Through our families, we receive love through the heroic sacrifices of others to find the faith and courage needed to become our best selves. God pours out His invisible grace for us through all the empowering love we receive over our lifetime whether we realize it or not. We may not believe in God during the hard times, but God believes in us even as we become dilapidated like 'The African Queen" towards the end of our lives that brings us all up to the finish line to fight a good fight against evil to celebrate God's goodness.

www.ingramcontent.com/pod-product-compliance
Lightning Source LLC
LaVergne TN
LVHW041941070526
838199LV00051BA/2870